Caribbean Poetry Now

Second Edition

Edited by Stewart Brown

Foreword by Mervyn Morris

Edward Arnold
A division of Hodder & Stoughton
LONDON NEW YORK MELBOURNE AUCKLAND

This anthology is dedicated to Anson
Gonzalez in awe of his achievements with
The New Voices.

© 1984, 1992 Selection and editorial matter Stewart Brown

First published in Great Britain 1984
Second edition 1992

Distributed in the USA by Routledge, Chapman and Hall, Inc.
29 West 35th Street, New York, NY 10001

British Library Cataloguing in Publication Data

Caribbean Poetry Now. – 2 Rev. ed
  I. Brown, Stewart
  811

  ISBN 0-340-57379-1

Typeset in Linotron Times by Rowland Phototypesetting Limited,
Bury St Edmunds, Suffolk
Printed and bound in Great Britain for Edward Arnold, a division
of Hodder and Stoughton Limited, Mill Road, Dunton Green,
Sevenoaks, Kent TV13 2YA by Biddles Limited, Guildford and
King's Lynn

CONTENTS

1: *Roots*

2: *Childhood and Adolescence*

3: *Folks*

4: *One Love*

5: *Home—City Life*

6: *Home—Country Life*

7: *Old Folks, Death and Grief*

8: *Gods, Ghosts and Spirits*

9: *Her Story*

10: *Exile and Homecoming*

ACKNOWLEDGEMENTS

For permission to use copyright material in this book, the editor and publishers would like to thank the following: the author for 'For My Daughter Yansan Yashoda' by John Agard; by kind permission of John Agard c/o Caroline Sheldon Literary Agency 'Wind and River Romance from *Lovelines for a Goat-born Lady* published by Serpent's Tail (1990) and 'Stereotype' from *Mangoes and Bullets* published by Pluto Press (1985); the author for 'Truth and Consequences' by Edward Baugh; the author for 'Back to Africa' and 'Rollin'-Calf' by Louise Bennett; New Beacon Books Ltd for the poems 'Early Innocence' and 'Fractured Circles' from *Fractured Circles* (1979). 'Dialogue Between Two Large Village Women' and 'Cut-way Feelins' from *Lucy's Letters and Loving* (1982) by James Berry; the author for 'Thinking Back on Yard Time' by James Berry; 'Simple Tings' and Soun De Abeng Fi Nanny' from '*Riddym Ravings And Other Poems*' by Jean Binta Breeze. Published by Race Today Publications. ISBN 0 947716 14 9. Price: £3.50 paperback; Bogle-L'Ouverture Publications Ltd for the poem 'Trench Town Shock' from *Touch Mi: Tell Mi* by Valerie Bloom; 'Return 1' © 1990 by Dionne Brand. Reprinted from *No Language Is Neutral* by permission of Coach House Press; Oxford University Press for the poems 'Lix' from *Mother Poem* (1977), 'Ancestors' and 'Ogun' from *Islands* (1969), 'Korabra' from *Masks* (1968), 'Batto', 'The Fisherman' and 'Indigone' from *Sun Poem* (1982) by Edward Kamau Brathwaite; 'Mai Village' © Edward Kamau Brathwaite 1987. Reprinted from *X/Self* by Edward Kamau Brathwaite (1987) by permission of Oxford University Press; Andre Deutsch Ltd for the poems 'Red Hills' and 'The Tourists' from *On the Coast* by Wayne Brown; 'Ramon Remembers' from *Voyages* by Wayne Brown. Inprint Caribbean Limited— Publisher; the author for 'When He Went Away' by Peggy Carr; New Beacon Books Ltd for the poems 'University of Hunger' and 'The Child Ran Into the Sea' from *Poems of Succession* (1977) and 'Rice' by Martin Carter; the author for 'Legend' by Faustin Charles; the author for 'Country Days' by Willi Chen; the author for 'Without Apology to Proust' by Christine Craig; Chatto and Windus Ltd for 'Airy Hall Iconography' from *Airy Hall* (1989) by Fred d'Aguiar; Dangaroo Press for 'Coolie Odyssey' by David Dabydeen, from *Coolie Odyssey* (1990); Peepal Tree Press, Leeds for 'Sonnet to New Flowers' and 'Oars' from *Bones* (1988) by Mahadai Das; the author for 'No Man's Land' by Gloria Escoffery; the author for 'Parish Registers' by John Gilmore; the author for 'A Fairy Tale' by Anson Gonzalez; the author for 'For My Mother' by Lorna Goodison; New Beacon Books Ltd for 'I Am Becoming My Mother' from *I Am Becoming My Mother* (1986) by Lorna Goodison; the author for 'Sunday Crosses' by Jean Goulbourne; the author for 'Caribbean Journal' by Cecil Gray; the author for 'Sun Poem XV' by Wilson Harris; the author for 'Albert' and 'Hot Summer Sunday' by A. L. Hendriks; the author for 'Origins' by Kendel Hippolyte; the author for 'Mek Dream Tek Yu Life' by Richard Ho Lung; the author for 'The Loaded Dice' by Amryl Johnson; the author for 'When Moon Shine' by Paul Keens Douglas; the author for

'Sad Mother Ballad' by Jane King; the author for 'Youtman' by Linton Kwesi Johnson; the author for 'Ground' and 'Moments' by John Robert Lee; the author for 'Yusman Ali, Charcoal Seller', 'Pelting Bees', 'Decorated for a Kiss' and 'On an Evening Turned to Rain' by Ian McDonald; 'Nurse Guyadeen and the Preacher' from 'Mercy Ward' by Ian McDonald (Peterloo Poets, 1988); the author for 'Arawak Prologue' by Basil McFarlane; the author for 'Saint Ras', 'Ad. for a Housing Scheme', and 'Hello Ungod' by Anthony McNeill; Dangaroo Press for 'Porknocker' by Mark McWatt from *Interiors* (1989); the author for 'Routine' by Malik; the author for 'Mammie' by E. A. Markham and 'The Sea' by E. A. Markham from *Human Rites: Selected Poems 1970–1982* published by Anvil Press in 1984; Dangaroo Press for 'Mixed' by Pauline Melville from *Rented Rooms*, ed., David Dabydeen 1988; Peepal Tree Press Leeds for 'Creole Gang' and 'Moon-gaza' from Koker (1987) by Rooplal Monar; the author for 'Wednesday Chronicle' by Pamela Mordecai; New Beacon Books Ltd for the poems 'Family Pictures' and 'For a Son' from *The Pond* (1973) and 'Terminal' from *Shadowboxing* (1979) by Mervyn Morris; the author for 'Aerogramme' by Philip Nanton; the author for 'Those Women' by Grace Nichols; 'Of Course When They Ask For Poems About The "Realities" of Black Women' and 'Wherever I Hang' from *Lazy Thoughts of A Lazy Woman* by Grace Nichols, published by Virago Press Limited (1989) and reproduced with their permission © 1989 Grace Nichols; and with the permission of Curtis Brown (London); Savacou and the author for 'Fewcha Gaan' by Fred Nunes; the author for 'Wasting Time' by Opal Palmer; Peepal Tree Press, Leeds for 'Crown Point' from *Crown Point* (1988) by Velma Pollard; The New Voices for the poems 'Shop', 'Downbeat' and 'Couvade' by Victor D. Questel; the author for 'Still My Teacher' by Rajandaye Ramkissoon-Chen; Mrs I. Roach for 'To My Mother' by her husband, E. Roach; the author for 'Theophilus Jones Walks Naked Down King Street' by Heather Royes; the author for 'Sweet Mango' by Andrew Salkey; the author for 'Uncle Time' by Dennis Scott; New Beacon Books ltd for the poems 'Guard-ring' and for Joy *Dreadwalk* by Denis Scott; Mrs Joy R. Scott for 'Ordering of Rooms' by her husband, Dennis Scott; Ian McDonald and Mrs Elma Seymour for 'There runs a dream' by her husband, A. J. Seymour; the author for 'Land of Look Behind' by Philip Sherlock; Mrs Nerissa Smith for 'Roots' and 'Mi C-YaaN beLieVe iT' by her son, Michael Smith; Jonathan Cape Ltd and the author for 'Ruins of a Great House', 'A Sea-Chantey' and 'A Letter for This Sunday' from *In a Green Night*, 'Names' from *Sea Grapes*, 'Laventille' from *The Castaway*, 'The Saddhu of Couva' and 'Shabine Encounters the Middle Passage' from 'The Schooner *Flight*' from *Star-Apple Kingdom* by Derek Walcott; Faber and Faber Ltd and the author for 'Midsummer, VII' from *Midsummer* by Derek Walcott.

Every effort has been made to trace and acknowledge ownership of copyright. The publishers will be glad to make suitable arrangements with any copyright holders whom it has not been possible to contact.

INTRODUCTION

This new edition of *Caribbean Poetry Now* retains all the poems that
were in the original and adds half as many again. Almost a decade
on from putting that first edition together it seemed time for an
updating and expansion of the anthology, reflecting both the new
voices who had emerged in that period and the recent work of more
established figures like Walcott, Brathwaite, Dennis Scott and Ian
McDonald. Poems have been added to all the original theme groups
and two new themes have been introduced—"Her Story", a
selection of poems by and about the experience of women in the
Caribbean, and "Exile and Homecoming"—a group of poems
reflecting the continuing concern of West Indian writers with those
"facts" of West Indian life. As in the original edition the
themes have been very broadly interpreted to include a wide range
of stylistic approaches. The presence of so many new women
poets—Jean Binta Breeze, Olive Senior, Merle Collins, etc.—and
the appearance of a group of poets of East Indian background—
David Dabydeen, Mahadia Das, Rooplal Monar and others—add a
distinctive range of voice and emphasis to the collection as a whole.
    The teaching apparatus at the end of the anthology—the notes
and questions—has been completely revised. The major change has
been to introduce questions that will encourage the students' own
creativity in response to the poems. After the "traditional"
questions which ask the student to read the poem more carefully
and think about how it works, there is a question which tries to
engage the student's imagination and lead him/her into making their
own experiments with creative writing. I am more and more
convinced—by my own practice as both teacher and poet—that the
"hands on" approach to poetry teaching is the most effective way to
get students to engage with the ideas, techniques and pleasures of
poetry. By trying to write themselves, trying to achieve different
effects and trying to apply different techniques, the students come
to a much better understanding of how poetry works. I have tried to
construct questions which will direct the students into different
kinds of writing—stories, passages of dialogue, biographical
sketches, newspaper-style articles, a piece of advertising copy, a
song lyric, letters, proverbs, a defence lawyer's speech (!)—but
mostly various kinds of poems . . . Sometimes I have asked the
student's to try and use the poem in the anthology as a kind of
template, sometimes I have picked up on an idea or image or use of

language in the poems to start the students off. Occasionally I have just given them the space—and licence—to respond to the poem in whatever way their imagination takes them. I hope that students will find this writing fun, I'm sure that they will learn a great deal just by trying and I'm confident that the effect of constructing their own anthologies of *Caribbean Poetry Now* will be to make "poetry" seem a much less daunting, difficult and dreaded subject.

Finally, I should like to acknowledge the advice and practical help of the following people: Mervyn Morris, for his generous and encouraging response to the whole project, Anne Walmsley and Howard Williams for allowing me access to their respective "archives" and for much valuable advice; Cilla, Douglas and Ceridwen Brown, Paulo Farias, Sarah Haley, Ron Narain, Monica Payne, Paul Shallcross, Ned Thomas, Jennie Walters and June Young for help with particular references and chores; Jenny Hall for her meticulous and sensitive editorial work; and Philip Walters of Edward Arnold for managing to be both imaginative *and* hard headed enough to transform a wild idea into a wild anthology.

Stewart Brown
1992

FOREWORD

I like the range and freshness of Stewart Brown's anthology. A stimulating mix, it brings together writers of established reputation and some whose names are less familiar (but who have often been writing well for years). Alongside such classics of Caribbean poetry as 'The Dust', 'Ruins of a Great House' and 'University of Hunger', it offers work from recent volumes (such as Derek Walcott's *The Star-apple Kingdom*, Martin Carter's *Poems of Affinity*, Edward Kamau Brathwaite's *Sun Poem*, James Berry's *Lucy's Letters and Loving* Dennis Scott's *Dreadwalk*) and much previously uncollected material.

Designed to help candidates prepare for the CXC English B Examination, the anthology is arranged thematically. The poems talk to each other—and not only within the individual sections. The teaching questions should assist, but cannot replace, the classroom teacher.

Some of these poems seem to invite or require performance. They become more fully available if we can hear them accurately spoken in the appropriate regional accent. Some have already been recorded; many more could usefully be made available on cassette. Hearing the poems may be of assistance not only, as is obvious, for poems by Oku Onuora, Malik, the late Mikey Smith, Richard Ho Lung, James Berry, John Figueroa, Fred Nunes, Anthony Hinkson, for example, but also for many poems that may at first seem sufficiently expressed in print. I mean items such as Brathwaite's 'Indigone' and the extract from Walcott's 'The Schooner *Flight*'.

The anthology inhabits many areas in the language continuum available to West Indian poets. It moves freely between regional variations of Standard English and Creole—Guyanese, Jamaican, Barbadian, Trinidadian, and so on. There is variety too in the detail of cultural reference: we encounter Indian religion, classical mythology, Jamaican and Guyanese folklore, for example. Students who feel immediately at home with poems from their own corner of the region will also find here poems reminding them that there is much to learn of life and art in other Caribbean territories and of a wider international heritage which Caribbean writers also own.

Mervyn Morris
January 1984

1
Roots

NAMES
Derek Walcott

for Edward Brathwaite

I

My race began as the sea began,
with no nouns, and with no horizon,
with pebbles under my tongue,
with a different fix on the stars.

5 But now my race is here,
in the sad oil of Levantine eyes,
in the flags of the Indian fields,

I began with no memory,
I began with no future,
10 but I looked for that moment
when the mind was halved by a horizon,

I have never found that moment
when the mind was halved by a horizon
for the goldsmith from Benares,

15 the stone-cutter from Canton,
as a fishline sinks, the horizon
sinks in the memory.

Have we melted into a mirror,
leaving our souls behind?
20 The goldsmith from Benares,
the stone-cutter from Canton,
the bronzesmith from Benin.

A sea-eagle screams from the rock,
and my race began like the osprey
25 with that cry,
that terrible vowel,
that I!

Behind us all the sky folded,
as history folds over a fishline,
30   and the foam foreclosed
with nothing in our hands

but this stick
to trace our names on the sand
which the sea erased again, to our indifference.

II

35   And when they named these bays
bays,
was it nostalgia or irony?

In the uncombed forest,
in uncultivated grass
40   where was there elegance
except in their mockery?
Where were the courts of Castille,
Versailles' colonnades
supplanted by cabbage palms
45   with Corinthian crests,
belittling diminutives,
then, little Versailles
meant plans for a pigsty,
names for the sour apples
50   and green grapes
of their exile.

Their memory turned acid
but the names held,
Valencia glows
55   with the lanterns of oranges,
Mayaro's
charred candelabra of cocoa.
Being men, they could not live
except they first presumed
60   the right of every thing to be a noun.
The African acquiesced,
repeated, and changed them

Listen, my children, say:
moubain: the hogplum,
65   *cerise*:   the wild cherry,
baie-la: the bay,
with the fresh green voices
they were once themselves
in the way the wind bends
70   our natural inflections.

These palms are greater than Versailles,
for no man made them,
their fallen columns greater than Castille,
no man unmade them
75   except the worm, who has no helmet,
but was always the emperor,

and children, look at these stars
over Valencia's forest!

Not Orion,
80   not Betelgeuse,
tell me, what do they look like?
Answer, you damned little Arabs!
Sir, fireflies caught in molasses.

ROOTS
Michael Smith

Roots
Roots
Roots

5   Lawwwwwwd
       an dem a roots
       an dem a roots

Roots

Youtman dem searchin
de crevices an corners
10   fi dem roots

       Lawwwwwwd
       an dem a roots
       an dem a roots

But searchin fi im roots
15   a cause an explosion
between man and man

       Lawwwwwwd
       but dem a roots
       but dem a roots

20   Some a sey
which roots
when de only roots dem can trace
start wid dem madda
an end wid dem granmadda

25   dem na roots
       Lawwwwwwd
       dem na roots

But youtman
rootin in de muck like
                    trenton
30   cause nobody never did tell im
whe im come from
so im a fi a root
fi fine out whe im a go

       Lawwwwwwd
35   an dem a roots
       an dem a roots

Intellect
a search fi im roots
through science

40   An dem a roots
       Lawwwwwwd
       an dem a roots

Odders a wear dashiki
sport Afro
45   locks head
smoke illy
fi identify wid dem roots

       Lawwwwwwd
       an dem a roots

50   Lawd
dem itical
rootical
ina dem physical

Some a beat drum
55   fi get closer to dem roots

       an dem a beat
       an dem a beat
       an dem a chant
       an dem a chant

60   Jah
Jah
Rastafari
Jah
Jah
65   Roots are I

       Lawwwwwwd
       an dem a roots
       an dem a roots

But look at dis one

70 Dem ax him whe im age
    Im sey roots
Sex?
    Roots
Name?
75   Nuh roots
cause dat nuh belongs to I an I

Some cursin dem roots
shoutin name like
wild
80 barbarian
savage
inhuman

What happen?
Fi dem roots
85 nuh humanitarian?

    Lawwwwwwd
    an dem a roots
    an dem a roots

90 t'accept dem blackness
t'accept dem blackness
t'accept dem blackness

an others
an others
as they are
95 as they are

Black man
Chinese man
Coolie man
White man
100 de whole a dem
a look fi dem
roots

    Lawwwwwwd
    an dem a roots
105   an dem a roots

UNIVERSITY OF HUNGER
Martin Carter

---

is the university of hunger the wide waste.
is the pilgrimage of man the long march.
The print of hunger wanders in the land.
The green tree bends above the long forgotten.
5 The plains of life rise up and fall in spasms.
The huts of men are fused in misery.

They come treading in the hoofmarks of the mule
passing the ancient bridge
the grave of pride
10 the sudden flight
the terror and the time.

They come from the distant village of the flood
passing from middle air to middle earth
in the common hours of nakedness.

15 Twin bars of hunger mark their metal brows
twin seasons mock them
parching drought and flood.

is the dark ones
the half sunken in the land.
20   is they who had no voice in the emptiness
in the unbelievable
in the shadowless.

They come treading on the mud floor of the year
mingling with dark heavy waters
25   and the sea sound of the eyeless flitting bat.
O long is the march of men and long is the life
and wide is the span.
is air dust and the long distance of memory
is the hour of rain when sleepless toads are silent
30   is broken chimneys smokeless in the wind
is brown trash huts and jagged mounds of iron.

They come in long lines toward the broad city
is the golden moon like a big coin in the sky
is the floor of bone beneath the floor of flesh
35   is the beak of sickness breaking on the stone
O long is the march of men and long is the life
and wide is the span
O cold is the cruel wind blowing.
O cold is the hoe in the ground.
40   They come like sea birds
flapping in the wake of a boat
is the torture of sunset in purple bandages
is the powder of fire spread like dust in the twilight
is the water melodies of white foam on wrinkled sand.

45   The long streets of night move up and down
baring the thighs of a woman
and the cavern of generation.
The beating drum returns and dies away.
The bearded men fall down and go to sleep.
50   The cocks of dawn stand up and crow like bugles.

is they who rose early in the morning
watching the moon die in the dawn.
is they who heard the shell blow and the iron clang
is they who had no voice in the emptiness
55   in the unbelievable
in the shadowless.
O long is the march of men and long is the life
and wide is the span.

THE LAND OF LOOK BEHIND
Philip Sherlock

The chase stopped here
at this harsh border-line
where tangled undergrowth and green-fringed
parapets of rock define
5   a freedom-fortress place,
the Land of Look Behind.

The chase stopped here,
the lean-ribbed hunting dogs
with hanging scarlet tongues, the driven slaves,
10   the armed militia men intent
to capture or to kill,
the red-necked overseer with darting mongoose eyes,
eyes searching for a running slave,
a piece of merchandise broke loose,
15   a man for freedom bound;
all bondsmen in pursuit,
to catch and cage a man gone free.

No land for living this,
no ordered fields astir with folk
20   obedient to the bull-horn's note,
nor curling smoke from mountain grounds
where men go free for half a day,
nor Great House talk, nor horologue of sounds
that mark the day's routine, the horn at dawn,
25   the creaking wagon wheels
the shrill-voiced pickney-gang
the bustle of the noon-day meal,
the curfew bell,
the lowing cattle penned at night. No stir
30   of jasmine-scented mountain breeze,
nor watchman's tread nor silent warmth of sleep.
No land for living this, with fissured rocks
and hostile crags, its limestone pinnacles honed sharp
by wind and rain,
35   shrub-shrouded deep ravines
ghost-tenanted at noon,
where moving feet no imprint make,
a breathless place of watching eyes
and ears that measure every sound.

40 The chase stopped here. The big boss-man
brick-red with sun and rage
with shaking fist his curses cried
and fouled the air with hate:
"Had I but known by cock-crow time,
45 had they but brought me word
by dawning time of your escape
I would by now have taken you
a tied and beaten thing, but still my own
with silver pieces bought.
50 That day aboard the ship
your gaze I felt upon me,
you held your head as though a man,
nor turned aside your eyes,
and counting out the cash I swore
55 to tame you as I would a horse,
to dull those proud rebellious eyes,
with treadmill, whip and iron chains
to break you to my will.
Now fled beyond my reach
60 to this accursed place
I yet will track you down
with magic and with Obi's might.
Come Bashra come, work fast your spells,
like feathered shafts my curses wing
65 with hate: black scum of earth
may hunger knot your guts,
your skin to parchment turn
with ravening thirst, may John Crows pluck
your eyes before you die,
70 your bones unburied lie,
your spirit never rest but tortured still
my burning curses bear."

The cursing died away.
The dogs, the limping slaves, the men
75 with muskets cold their steps retraced
and like a gently moving tide
the tepid stillness washed away
the foulness from the day.

To him who panting lay concealed
80 beneath the mountain cedar's shade
the night brought stars and healing calm
and fears new-born of what the dawn might bring.

To him alone and in distress
Lubola spoke, a presence from the shades,
85   who first with his Maroons the mountains claimed:
"Take courage, Brother Man,
your brothers round you stand
to comfort and sustain,
ancestral spirits who have gained
90   a wider sphere than mortals know
yet tied as by a naval-string
to living kith and kin,
each with his own, his special place,
a rock, a mountain cedar tree,
95   a cavern deep, a spring, a shrine
where we, the living past, commune,
where spirits speak to mortals through
a burning bush, a flight of birds,
a falling branch, a thunderclap
100   when skies are clear.
Like you we chose the mountain road,
chose hunger, nakedness and thirst,
we learned to find in this dry land
the secret springs in hidden caves
105   to hunt the wild pigs, track the conies shy,
as allies use the trees and birds
the stirring leaf that danger warned,
the wind that told of manhunts near,
and now a silent host we guard
110   the living with our power.
From this time forth, Maroon,
we compass you about,
we who the Spanish power broke
we who refused the English yoke,
115   protect you here, unseen unheard.
Take comfort, Brother Man, no whip
no curse can touch you here,
you rest secure in this your home,
this freedom Land of Look Behind".

120   When first the darkness from the sky
began to pass
a darker shape itself revealed
beside the cedar's trunk
and Cudjoe spoke,

125 his low-pitched voice like distant organ-pipes:
"From this time forth you are with us,
you are with us and we with you.
We offer you no ease, no rest,
but we will teach you how to live
130 and keep the freedom we have won,
to find the water springs, to speak
the language of the Goombay drum,
the Coromanti flute to play
whose plaintive fading note deceives
135 the lonely Mountain Witch.
Each day each night
will bring its task, the slashing raid
with cutlass and with flame,
the canefields all ablaze, and women seized
140 to bear us sons, with corn and meat
and store of arms to keep us free. With us
in hidden ambuscades you seem
a shrub, a branch with Maroon wiss entwined,
and at the Abeng's note you wake
145 and kill without a sound,
nor mercy seek nor mercy give.
My eyes are far beyond this place,
my ears in distant towns. News comes
of musters of militia men,
150 of red-coats landing fresh from home
of Cuban bloodhounds and their trainers brought
to hunt us down. This is our life.
Our children hear no talk of peace,
their games are skills that keep us free,
155 each year brings its alarms, its bloody toll.
We do not yield. We pay the price
that freedom takes.
This cedar tree that sheltered you
is now your birth-cord tree,
160 your naval-string is here
and you will bear from this day forth
the day-name Quamin that you bore
beside the Volta's stream
in your ancestral land.

165 These brooding jagged rocks, these trees,
the bitter damsel and wild tamarind
with scarlet twisted pod,
the Quassia with pointed leaves
the greenheart and the bulletwood,
170 these are our revelation-place,
from each, as once in Ghana far away
the spirits speak, Funtumi here
and here Kodia strong,
the spirit of the cedar tree.
175 Here your ancestral spirits live
Up Quamin come,
and claim your freedom land,
The Land of Look Behind".

CREOLE GANG
Rooplal Monar

Baling and throwing
among green canes from rusty punts,
their sweated faces
show how many days and nights have passed
5 between cane roots and black streams,
sunburnt trashes and parched earth,
wearied days and restless reality.
Their hands and limbs are but fragments
that walk and bathe,
10 when sun shines, rains fall
and drivers shout.
Who can tell when midday meets
their rest—they eat, they talk?
Their limbs cry and hearts burn.
15 Is this not the century of dreams,
of tales told by ancestors
of a faith told by life?
Again and again they will bale and throw
curse and rest among green canes
20 and black earth, wishing, wishing . . .

TO MY MOTHER
Eric Roach

It is not long, not many days are left
Of the dead sun, nights of the crumbled moon;
Nor far to go; not all your roads of growth,
Love, grief, labour of birth and bone
5   And the slow slope from the blood's noon
Are shorter than this last.

And it is nothing. Only the lusty heroes
And those whose summer's sweet with lust
And wine and roses fear. The children do not;
10   Theirs is young Adam's innocence.
The old do not; they welcome the earth's suction
And the bone's extinction into rock.

The image of your beauty growing green,
Your bone's adolescence I could not know,
15   Come of your middle years, your July loins.
I found you strong and tough as guava scrub,
Hoeing the growing, reaping the ripe corn;
Kneading and thumping the thick dough for bread.

And now you're bowed, bent over to the ground;
20   An old gnarled tree, all her bows drooped
Upon the cross of death, you crawl up
Your broken stairs like Golgotha, and all the dead
Beckon your dying bones . . .

I do not mourn, but all my love
25   Praise life's continuity the endless year.
I see death broken at each seed's rebirth.
My poems labour from your blood
As all my mind burns on our peasant stock
That cannot be consumed till time is killed.

30   Oh, time's run past the time your hands made bread
To this decrepitude; but in the stream
Of time I watch the stone, the image
Of my mother making bread my boyhood long,
Mossed by the crusty memories of bread.
35   Oh may my art grow whole as her hands' craft.

ANCESTORS
Edward Kamau Brathwaite

I

Every Friday morning my grandfather
left his farm of canefields, chickens, cows,
and rattled in his trap down to the harbour town
to sell his meat. He was a butcher.
5 Six-foot-three and very neat: high collar,
winged, a grey cravat, a waistcoat, watch-
chain just above the belt, thin narrow-
bottomed trousers, and the shoes his wife
would polish every night. He drove the trap
10 himself: slap of the leather reins
along the horse's back and he'd be off
with a top-hearted homburg on his head:
black English country gentleman.

Now he is dead. The meat shop burned,
15 his property divided. A doctor bought
the horse. His mad alsatians killed it.
The wooden trap was chipped and chopped
by friends and neighbours and used to stop-
gap fences and for firewood. One yellow
20 wheel was rolled across the former cowpen gate.
Only his hat is left. I "borrowed" it.
I used to try it on and hear the night wind
man go battering through the canes, cocks waking up and thinking
it was dawn throughout the clinking country night.
25 Great caterpillar tractors clatter down
the broken highway now; a diesel engine grunts
where pigs once hunted garbage.
A thin asthmatic cow shares the untrashed garage.

II

All that I can remember of his wife,
30 my father's mother, is that she sang us songs
("Great Tom Is Cast" was one), that frightened me.
And she would go chug chugging with a jar
of milk until its white pap turned to yellow
butter. And in the basket underneath the stairs
35 she kept the polish for grandfather's shoes.

All that I have of her is voices:
laughing me out of fear because a crappaud
jumped and splashed the dark where I was huddled
in the galvanized tin bath; telling us stories
40 round her fat white lamp. It was her Queen
Victoria lamp, she said; although the stamp
read Ever Ready. And in the night, I listened to her singing
in a Vicks and Vapour Rub-like voice what you would call the blues

III

Com-a look
45 come-a look
see wha' happen

come-a look
come-a look
see wha' happen

50 Sookey dead
Sookey dead
Sookey dead-o

Sookey dead
Sookey dead
55 Sookey dead-o.

Him a-wuk
him a-wuk
till 'e bleed-o

him a-wuk
60 him a-wuk
till 'e bleed-o

Sookey dead
Sookey dead
Sookey dead-o

65 Sookey dead
Sookey dead
Sookey dead-o . . .

OGUN
Edward Kamau Brathwaite

My uncle made chairs, tables, balanced doors on, dug out
coffins, smoothing the white wood out

with plane and quick sandpaper until
it shone like his short-sighted glasses.

5   The knuckles of his hands were sil-
vered knobs of nails hit, hurt and flat-

tened out with blast of heavy hammer. He was knock-knee'd, flat-
footed and his clip clop sandals slapped across the concrete

flooring of his little shop where canefield mulemen and a fleet
10   of Bedford lorry drivers dropped in to scratch themselves and talk.

There was no shock of wood, no beam
of light mahogany his saw teeth couldn't handle.

When shaping squares for locks, a key hole
care tapped rat tat tat upon the handle

15   of his humpbacked chisel. Cold
world of wood caught fire as he whittled: rectangle

window frames, the intersecting x of fold-
ing chairs, triangle

trellises, the donkey
20   box-cart in its squeaking square.

But he was poor and most days he was hungry.
Imported cabinets with mirrors, formica table

tops, spine-curving chairs made up of tubes, with hollow
steel-like bird bones that sat on rubber ploughs,

25   thin beds, stretched not on boards, but blue high-tensioned cables,
were what the world preferred.

And yet he had a block of wood that would have baffled them.
With knife and gimlet care he worked away at this on Sundays,

explored its knotted hurts, cutting his way
30   along its yellow whorls until his hands could feel

how it had swelled and shivered, breathing air,
its weathered green burning to rings of time,

its contoured grain still tuned to roots and water.
And as he cut, he heard the creak of forests:

35   green lizards faces gulped, grey memories with moth
eyes watched him from their shadows, soft

liquid tendrils leaked among the flowers
and a black rigid thunder he had never heard within his hammer

came stomping up the trunks. And as he worked within his
40   shattered
Sunday shop, the wood took shape: dry shuttered

eyes, slack anciently everted lips, flat
ruined face, eaten by pox, ravaged by rat

and woodworm, dry cistern mouth, cracked
45   gullet crying for the desert, the heavy black

enduring jaw; lost pain, lost iron;
emerging woodwork image of his anger.

RUINS OF A GREAT HOUSE
Derek Walcott

though our longest sun sets at right
declensions and makes but winter
arches, it cannot be long before we
lie down in darkness, and have our
light in ashes . . .
BROWNE: URN BURIAL

Stones only, the *disjecta membra* of this Great House,
Whose moth-like girls are mixed with candledust,
Remain to file the lizard's dragonish claws;
The mouths of those gate cherubs streaked with stain.
5   Axle and coachwheel silted under the muck
Of cattle droppings.
                Three crows flap for the trees,
And settle, creaking the eucalyptus boughs,
A smell of dead limes quickens in the nose
10   The leprosy of Empire.
              "Farewell, green fields"
              "Farewell, ye happy groves!"

Marble as Greece, like Faulkner's south in stone,
Deciduous beauty prospered and is gone;
15   But where the lawn breaks in a rash of trees
A spade below dead leaves will ring the bone
Of some dead animal or human thing
Fallen from evil days, from evil times.

It seems that the original crops were limes
20   Grown in the silt that clogs the river's skirt;
The imperious rakes are gone, their bright girls gone,
The river flows, obliterating hurt.

I climbed a wall with the grill ironwork
Of exiled craftsmen, protecting that great house
25   From guilt, perhaps, but not from the worm's rent,
Nor from the padded cavalry of the mouse.
And when a wind shook in the limes I heard
What Kipling heard; the death of a great empire, the abuse
Of ignorance by Bible and by sword.

30   A green lawn, broken by low walls of stone
     Dipped to the rivulet, and pacing, I thought next
     Of men like Hawkins, Walter Raleigh, Drake,
     Ancestral murderers and poets, more perplexed
     In memory now by every ulcerous crime.
35   The world's green age then was a rotting lime
     Whose stench became the charnel galleon's text.

     The rot remains with us, the men are gone.
     But, as dead ash is lifted in a wind,
     That fans the blackening ember of the mind,
40   My eyes burned from the ashen prose of Donne.

     Ablaze with rage I thought,
     Some slave is rotting in this manorial lake,
     And still the coal of my compassion fought:
     That Albion too, was once
45   A colony like ours, "Part of the continent, piece of the main"
     Nook-shotten, rook o'er blown, deranged
     By foaming channels, and the vain expense
     Of bitter faction.

                    All in compassion ends
50   So differently from what the heart arranged:
     "as well as if a manor of thy friend's . . ."

BACK TO AFRICA
Louise Bennett

Back to Africa, Miss Mattie?
Yuh no know what yuh dah seh?
Yuh haffi come from somewhe fus
Before yuh go back deh!

5   Me know seh dat yuh great great great
Granma was African,
But Mattie, doan yuh great great great
Granpa was Englishman?

Den yuh great granmodder fader
10 By yuh fader side was Jew?
An yuh grampa by yuh modder side
Was Frenchie parlez-vous?

But de balance a yuh family,
Yuh whole generation,
15 Oonoo all bawn dung a Bung Grung—
Oonoo all is Jamaican!

Den is weh yuh gwine, Miss Mattie?
Oh, yuh view de countenance,
An between yuh an de Africans
20 Is great resemblance!

Ascorden to dat, all dem blue-yeye
White American
Who-for great granpa was Englishman
Mus go back to Englan!

25 What a debil of a bump-an-bore,
Rig-jig an palam-pam
Ef de whole worl start fi go back
Whe dem great grampa come from!

Ef a hard time yuh dah run from
30 Teck yuh chance! But Mattie, do,
Sure a whe yuh come from so yuh got
Somewhe fi come back to!

Go a foreign, seek yuh fortune,
But no tell nobody seh
35 Yuh dah go fi seek yuh homelan,
For a right deh so yuh deh!

origins
Kendel Hippolyte

from the O of darkness
whole and heavy with itself
feeling in its density a pulse, the moan of first light
the yearn of nothing strending to know itself
5   in things, the hurt and hungering of being
all of all that time only
an O, an open mouth about to
scream :
from this we come, living

10   we are
warm fragments from the substance
of sun, meteoroid, the far-flung star.
still throbbing in our chest is
the first hurtling pain
15   that cracked the darkness heaven-wide open
shattering silence in a thunder-laugh of light.
all this agonies ago, long
before the first aeons,
before histories, long
20   before there was a time or Time

pieces now, fragile pieces
warm still
from first fire
this we are.
25   the heart exploding
momently, rehearses that creation
and the spark of word
lights our silence
to a bonfire of speech we gather round
30   seeing things by its light

until
seared from an inner burning
we crackle, flame
into humanity

ARAWAK PROLOGUE
Basil McFarlane

We cross many rivers, but here is no anguish; our
dugouts have straddled the salt sea. The land
we have found is a mountain, magical with birds'
throats, and in the sea are fish. In the forests are many
5   fleet canoes. And here is no anguish, though storms
still the birds and frighten the fish from inshore shallows. And
once it seemed the mountain moved, groaning
a little.
10   In the sunless wet, after
rains, leaves in the tangled underbrush (like cool hands
of children on face and arms) glisten. I
am not one for society, and think how the houses throb with the noise
of women up to their elbows
15   in cassava milk, when the dove-grey sea's breast is
soft in the lowering light—and the land we found
fairest of women.
                    That bright day, the light
like clusters of gold fruit, alone, unknown
20   of any, the dugout and I fled the shore's
burning beauty; the first wave's shock
an ecstasy like singing, oh, and the sea's strength
entered these arms. All day
we climbed the hill
25   of the sea.
            It seemed I died
and found that bleak
Coyaba of the wise. The dugout
faltered in a long smooth swell. There were houses on the
30   water, aglow with light and music and strange
laughter. Like great birds, with
ominous mutterings and preenings, they
hovered on every side. Flat on the dugout's
bottom, I prayed deliverance. Where was the land, the
35   houses throbbing with the noise of women
up to their elbows in cassava milk?
                    The towering birds
floated majestically on, dragging me a little in their
fabulous wake.
40   I tell this story in the evening, after
the smoke of pipes has addled the elders'
brains, and I am assured at least of the children's respectful
silence. I am no longer certain it happened to me.

2
Childhood and Adolescence

FOR MY DAUGHTER YANSAN YASHODA
John Agard

at two minutes past six
you screamed your wombsong coming
into a new world
of shape and sound

5   what brings you to these shores little one?
what dreams lie curled
in this your feathersoft fist
she who mothered you can never tell

what pains will touch your path
10   between the cradle and the grave
no one knows

but like the flower that grows
knowing not which wind
will one day uncomb its bloom
15   so must you my child

so sleep well little one
and dream your dream
before the price of sleep becomes too dear

CARIBBEAN JOURNAL
Cecil Gray

He stands outside the fencing looking in.

Inside sunbathers relishing their flesh—
some white, some black, and some of other skins—
diving and swimming feign not to notice him,
5   fingers of doubt spread wide, gripping the holes of mesh.

Some people on the grass are picknicking.

His pants are torn; he does not have a shirt;
his face, a mask of sun-flaked grease and dirt
too young to understand his day's events,

10   dreams mountain-slide of magic dollars and cents
     to cancel knowledge of the stomach's pain,
     eyes learning what will later reach his brain.

     In time they'll be afraid to hear his curse
     at god's unholy sunday-school arrangement,
15   put him inside a wire mesh, or worse,
     and sunbathe in the same sun on his hearse
     or perish if his bullet gets them first.

YOUTMAN
Linton Kwesi Johnson

     youtman,
     today is your day say di time is now.
     site? ovastan. youtman.
     check out di shape yu haffe faam;
5   mind who yu harm.

     youdauta,
     you are di queen of di day an di nite is your mite.
     site? overstan. youdauta.
     check out di tide before yu jump in di watah;
10   den swim, yea sing, sing youdauta.

     youtrebel,
     yu know bout di flame yu livin fire.
     yu know, youtrebel, yu livin fire.
     guide di flame fram di wheat to di tares;
15   watch dem burn an flee free

     fram yu kulcha,
     tek in di love say tek in di love.
     dont lay in di way dat will cause decay,
     an folly is di way of di fool.
20   site? youtman? scene. move on.

"BATTO"
(from SUN POEM)
Edward Kamau Brathwaite

I

Of all the boys on the beach batto was the biggest brave. best
swimmer best diver best floater he was the shark of the sea-egg
season and he ducked every boy he was sure he could beat any
time any place without reason

5 he was the shake of their cake the stone in their bush, he was
the boast of the beach-boys gang

batto came from the tumbledown village of low wooden
houses overlooking the bay which stood on their stilts like a
crab on its claws. where they nevvah had bottles rounn their
garden beds

10 caus they nevvah had gardens an bottles were fuh fights an
they was plenty plenty fights in de hickey. they could curse
yuh muddah an ax fuh yuh faddah cause they didnt have
mothers like the land-boys had an you couldnt curse they
fathers who were fishermen

15 batto never had a mother like the land-boys had and hed never
even had to go to school. but hed been to dodds and hoped
one day to go to a proper prison for the man would cross
his path so the beach-boys said

20 dodds was the place with the high barbed wire and the
cat-o-nine tails far far away in the country. but your parents
were vague if you asked where it was what it meant. you were
told it was the place where the bad boys went

II

when he was he didnt know how much then, batto had burss
another boy eye in a fight

25 it was so:

You does stann toe to toe knee to knee and does stare at each
     udder
wid a fowlcock eye
then one is step back on tro dung e cap an comman

30   touch dat

but you isnt to look at de tro dung cap
but get back position in de fowlcock eye.

now batto bad bad bad when it come to a fight
an dis boy was a poor-great fool

35   *so it happenin so:*

de boy get a stone in e hann how uh doan know how
an batto when um start start out empty

but e step back quick an tro dung e cap an comman
touch dat

40   *an de poor-great boy turn an look*
when quick quick quick as a hen does peck

batto ups wid uh rock dat e feel all de time by e foot
an den murder start

e tek a step back wid de rock in e ann
45   *an by de time de boy look back front*

batto bark drop dat
to de stone in de udder boy hann

but de fool boy move
mek to puff out e chess when

50   bam

batto rockstone lann in e eye
so they senn e to dodd for being out-

lorded an de blood dat e bring pun de udda boy eye
so the beach-boys said

THE CHILD RAN INTO THE SEA
Martin Carter

The child ran into the sea
but ran back from the waves, because
the child did not know the sea
on the horizon, is not the same sea
5   ravishing the shore.

What every child wants is always
in the distance; like the sea
on the horizon. While, on the shore
nearby, at the feet of every child
10   shallow water, eating the edges
of islands and continents does little more,
little more than foam like spittle
at the corners of the inarticulate mouth
of some other child who wants to run
15   into the sea, into the horizon.

A FAIRY TALE
Anson Gonzalez

Openly he says: Sir, when I grow up
I want to be a fine man; someone like you.
Secretly he says: You old fool, I'll join
a gang like Applejackers or Navarones
5   and if we catch you in the street
we will break all your bones.
You say you teach me about life
but you don't know that life is strife
between mother and father.

10   Life is nothing to eat when morning comes;
life is no money to buy books and uniforms.
No this, no that, no taking part
in so many things you say make life.
Life is a drunk father on payday,
15   and mother with her feller on Saturday.
Life is sickness and no cash for doctor.
What you teach as life is just a fairy tale.

MEK DREAM
TEK YU LIFE
Richard Ho Lung

Sea a swell, sun a flare,
wind a dance and weep a song;
rain a flood and man a kill
hide ina mi belly an hold mi hand.

5   Quiet, sweet pickney,
no cry ya,
scorpion kyah walk' 'nancy web,
mek dream tek yu life ya.

Coo pickney nurse mumma swell wid child
10   and puppa cut stinkin' toe walk ten mile;
see Abel catch wata a give to Cain
so dutty tough but it a rain.

Quiet, sweet pickney,
no cry ya
15   sleep, hush, hush,
mek dream tek yu life ya.

A hug dem head and kiss dem eye,
tickle dem navel dem scream a smile;
music a pound and weeping inside
20   and we sing out fi Jesus Chris'.

Sea swell,
sun flare,
rain flood,
man kill,
25   life!

Quiet, sweet pickney,
no cry ya
scorpion kyah walk 'nancy web,
mek dream tek yu life ya.

A LESSON FOR
THIS SUNDAY
Derek Walcott

The growing idleness of summer grass
With its frail kites of furious butterflies
Requests the lemonade of simple praise
In scansion gentler than my hammock swings
5   And rituals no more upsetting than a
Black maid shaking linen as she sings
The plain notes of some protestant hosanna
Since I lie idling from the thought in things,

Or so they should. Until I hear the cries
10   Of two small children hunting yellow wings,
Who break my sabbath with the thought of sin.
Brother and sister, with a common pin,
frowning like serious lepidopterists.
The little surgeon pierces the thin eyes.
15   Crouched on plump haunches, as a mantis prays
She shrieks to eviscerate its abdomen.
The lesson is the same. The maid removes
Both prodigies from their interest in science.
The girl, in lemon frock, begins to scream
20   As the maimed, teetering thing attempts its flight.
She is herself a thing of summery light,
Frail as a flower in this blue August air,
Not marked for some late grief that cannot speak.

The mind swings inward on itself in fear
25   Swayed towards nausea from each normal sign.
Heredity of cruelty everywhere,
And everywhere the frocks of summer torn,
The long look back to see where choice is born,
As summer grass sways to the scythe's design.

TRADITION
Anthony Hinkson

Put you han' to you mout', boy
when you gine cough
an' say excuse muh.
Say excuse muh or lemme knock
5   you block off.

                              Excuse muh.

Dah is wuh to say, boy,
dah is wuh to say.
You never grow too old
10   to learn dem manners
dat we learn in we day.
Manners mek de man . . .
an all dem little courtesies
yes, sir; no sir;
15   thank you man;
excuse me please
nobody never t'ought dat to say dem did a crime,
but—
today to be polite, boy,
20   is just a waste o' time.

People t'inkin too much bout money—
deed in fait' dey is—
you would never see a man tip he hat to a miss;
or stand up in de bus
25   so a lady could sit down . . .
an another lesson, boy, as you go long . . .
you is to be angry an sin not . . .

                         Achoo! achoo! achoo!

Christ
30   all you golf balls fly in muh face, boy.
You ain' know I would—

COLONIAL GIRL'S SCHOOL
Olive Senior

For Marlene Smith MacLeish

Borrowed images
willed our skins pale
muffled our laughter
lowered our voices
5   let out our hems
dekinked our hair
denied our sex in gym tunics and bloomers
harnessed our voices to madrigals
and genteel airs
10   yoked our minds to declensions in Latin
and the language of Shakespeare

> Told us nothing about ourselves
> There was nothing about us at all

How those pale northern eyes and
15   aristocratic whispers once erased us
How our loudness, our laughter
debased us

> There was nothing left of ourselves
> Nothing about us at all

20   Studying: *History Ancient and Modern*
Kings and Queens of England
Steppes of Russia
Wheatfields of Canada

> There was nothing of our landscape there
25   Nothing about us at all

Marcus Garvey turned twice in his grave.
'Thirty-eight was a beacon. A flame.
They were talking of desegregation
in Little Rock, Arkansas, Lumumba
30   and the Congo. To us mumbo-jumbo.
We had read Vachel Lindsay's
vision of the jungle

> Feeling nothing about ourselves
> There was nothing about us at all

35 Months, years, a childhood memorising
Latin declensions
(For our language
—"bad talking"—
detentions)

40　　Finding nothing about us there
　　Nothing about us at all

So, friend of my childhood years
One day we'll talk about
How the mirror broke
45 Who kissed us awake
Who let Anansi from his bag

For isn't it strange how
northern eyes
in the brighter world before us now

50 Pale?

MIXED
Pauline Melville

Sometimes, I think
My mother with her blue eyes
And flowered apron
Was exasperated
5 At having such a sallow child,
And my mulatto daddee
Silenced
By having such an English-looking one.

And so my mother
10 Rubbed a little rouge on my cheeks
For school,
Lest people should think
She was not doing her job properly.

And my father chose to stay at home
15 On sports days.

EARLY INNOCENCE
James Berry

Remorse never came near it
when we sank puppies and kittens
or when we whacked worms
to see how pieces wriggled.

5   It could have been called pure
how we tested birds-egg thinness
with knocks, and how we took
half full bags of fledglings
from summer woods.

10   Doubt came nowhere near
laughter ringing round us,
when we showed the sun
the weakling's willy, and made
the spastic boy eat dirt.

15   Nothing like trouble was about
when we caught and raced
the neighbour's pony, over
and over sultry pastureland
and swore with tears
20   the beast bathed in the pond.

But then early fun had not become
an expert's guide to living
to make the mute and the weak pay,
in jungle or city.

25   Every fish we hooked we cooked.
Every bird we shot was seasoned.

3
Folks

GUARD-RING
Dennis Scott

Moon shadow burning,
Watch where I walking, Lord.
Make mi foot step hard
on the enemy's shadow
5 an hear me.
    I wearing de ring dem tonight—
one gainst hate and de red pepper
tongue of malice, a snake-eye
bone-ring to touch
10 if I buck up de tempter,
one ring gainst love-me
an one gainst de finger of famine,
an one for the death by drowning,
an one from fire;
15 an a bright copper ring
that I fine in a fish belly,
tun me safe an salt
from de barracuta teet of desire.

But moon shadow falling.
20 I fraid for de shape of de winding—
de road too crooked,
it making a rope to twine me!
An Lord, I tired
to tell yu mi torment, but listen

25 an learn me, an reach me
to home.   I believe
in de blessed ring, but Chris'
I praising yu candle also,
I raising mi heart like a smalls,
30 like a coal that outing
to light it—
    guard me asleep an awake!
De ring did bless in de balm yard
but Thee I praise.
35 I singing out loud
for de hill dem to hear me an tremble
De Lord is my Shepherd,
I shall not fear!
I singing so loud, down to de moon
40 going shake, I crying out,
Chris' yu hear!
An de moonshine wetting mi face up
like oil of plenty.

I going alone to mi house
45 wid de ring pon mi finger,
but walk wid me ever
an ever, tree score an ten,
an de moon shall wet me,
de ring shall praise Thee and heal me
50 an de mout shall bless Thee
for ever, amen
Amen.

TRUTH AND CONSEQUENCES
Edward Baugh

When the mob swerved
at him
he screamed
"I'm not the man you're after.
5   I'm Cinna the poet.
I never meddled in politics!"

The mob knew better. "Then tear him,"
it screamed back, "tear him
for his bad verses!"

10   It was then he learned
too late
there's no such thing as "**only** literature."
Every line commits you.
Those you thought dead will rise,
15   accusing. And if you plead
you never meant them,
then feel responsibility
break on you in a sudden sweat
as the beast bears down.

THOSE WOMEN
Grace Nicols

Cut and contriving women
hauling fresh shrimps
up in their seines

standing waist deep
5   in the brown voluptuous
water of their own element

how I remember those women
sweeping in the childish rivers
of my eyes

10   and the fish slipping like
eels through their laughing thighs.

SHOP
Victor D Questel

Buzzing voices crying for Koo
drown the broken wind in the corner.
Lard. 4lb rice

two pound sugar. No salt this week.
5   Chop. Meat swings in the balance. A pig
raises his trotter for silence.

Mark all this on the account. Koo
does not trust the rumours of
prosperity. He too has his little
10   red book. His sabots have the sharp
clipped alertness of the march-song
of high finance.

One night Koo out off with the turn
of his Yale locks. Ram got wind of it.
15   The shop is now under new management.

The proud sign goes up—VEGETABLE DEPOT—
R. Rampersad. (No Credit).
Things aren't clearly priced.
Koo is in Toronto now;
20   and the Depot seldom has vegetables.

Lard; life dread.

SAINT RAS
Anthony McNeill

Every stance seemed crooked. He had
not learned to fall in with the straight
queued, capitalistic, for work.
He was uneasy in traffic.

5   One step from that intersection
could, maybe, start peace. But he dread-
fully missed, could never proceed
with the rest when the white signal

flashed safe journey. Bruised, elbowed-in
10   his spirits stopped at each crossing,
seeking the lights for the one sign
indicated to take him across

to the true island of Ras.
But outside his city of dreams
15   was no right-of-passage, it seemed.
Still-anchored by faith, he idled

inside his hurt harbour and even
his innocent queen posed red
before his poised, inchoate bed.
20   Now exiled more, or less,

he retracts his turgid divinity,
returns to harsh temporal streets
whose uncertain crossings reflect
his true country. Both doubt and light.

ROUTINE
Malik

CLOCK AND MOVE MAN!
CLOCK AND MOVE!
is eight hours now
I in hey
5   slaverin an
slaverin since
marnin since
marnin

CLOCK AND MOVE MAN!
10   CLOCK AND MOVE!
whole eight hours now
I in hey
labarin an
labarin since
15   marnin since
marnin

CLOCK AND MOVE MAN!
CLOCK AND MOVE!
is centuries now
20   I in hey!
all dem hours now
I in hey!
slaverin an
labarin since
25   marnin since
marnin

CLOCK AND MOVE MAN!
CLOCK AND MOVE!
Yes SIREEEEEE
30   de siren done blow
de siren done blow
till tomorrow
till
tomorrow.

WEDNESDAY CHRONICLE
Pam Mordecai

On Wednesday I fed the children
and dogs, consulted the almanac
on the time to plant cabbages
cleaned out the kitchen cabinets

5   A little damp

On Wednesday I fed the children
and dogs, cut my toenails and
observed that they were growing hard
I sneezed a lot

10   It threatened rain

On Wednesday I fed the children
and dogs, read the newspaper
deplored the state of the nation
and took my pills

15   An intermittent drizzle

On Wednesday I fed the children
and dogs. In the sink the dishes
teetered.   My hands were hot.

Rain . . . steady

20   On Wednesday I fed the children
and dogs and went to bed quite ill

Outside, a thunderstorm

On Wednesday
Skies clear
25   Consuming blue.

LIX
Edward Kamau Brathwaite

I

Chalkstick the teacher

dreamer of sundaes
screamer of adjverbs, latin
ablutive clauses, mad-

5   rigal grace notes

tinkled his bicycle bell
years after the invention of the v-8 ford

it was 8.05 in the morning

mohammet
10   had come to my mother's black
mountain

and although the traffic was rushing towards the junctions like blood
clots: sugar pressure varicose vein: he knew

that he had many more lies to live

15   it was plain that perhaps, who knows,
he might become a senior master
one day, or even a min-

ister: *let me not think on it*: shakes-
pear? even his face, god wot,
20   in plaster of paris on one o' them lib'ry
shelves: *hmmmm*: long hair wig: me lod
the chief josstice: wreath-
ing the recitation for services rendered in ass-

isting the pupils of the un-
25   ready to win book fair prizes, blow
their brains up, demolish express

trains trans-
porting the virgin of guadeloupe, spin
tops, become nobel wize winners

30   he was already forty
    married/un
    married cow-

    ard: living with
    a woe-

35   man who dusted his chin
    every born-

    in
    with baby's talcum pow-

    der: hate-
40   ing her: need-

    ing her daily as if
    she was maid for the job

II

    to build a nation of forked sticks
    to kill the blade in those dark mahoe bodies

45   to iron the devil out of their pants
    to see that they spit in tune

    that they don't clap their hands, shake their heads, tap their feet
    to the tam tom:

    let there be no ting-ling no shak-shak
50   no drum

    let them not stare from the whites of their eyes
    at idols they have never forgotten

    wear feathers
    push bones through each others' congolese nostrils

55   but to have them neatly arraigned in squares:
    packs packages the iron duke of wellington

    the noble duke of york

    as on the jesus ships of the faulked atlantic cross-
    age: like cabbages, like sardine kings and queens

60   to have them honour this mean-
    ness: knowing their place at the foot of the nation:
    backseat bus stop bellboy black

    no jonah deep sea wailing driver
    no daniels in the lions den
65   no martinlutherblazinpen

    just charlie chalkstick the teacher

YUSMAN ALI, CHARCOAL SELLER
Ian McDonald

Some men have lives of sweet and seamless gold.
No dent of dark or harshness mars those men.
Not Yusman Ali though, not that old charcoal man
Whose heart I think has learned to break a hundred times a day.
5   He rides his cart of embered wood in a long agony.

He grew rice and golden apples years ago
He made an ordinary living by the long mud shore,
Laughed and drank rum like any other man and planned his four sons' glory
His young eyes watched the white herons rise like flags
10   And the sun brightening on the morning water in his fields.
His life fell and broke like a brown jug on a stone.
In middle age his four sons drowned in one boat up a pleasant river,
The wife's heart cracked and Yusman Ali was alone, alone, alone.
Madness howled in his head. His green fields died.

15   He burns the wild wood in his barren yard alone,
Sells the charcoal on the villaged coast and feasts on stars at night.
Thinness makes a thousand bones around his scorched heart.
His Moon-scarred skin is sick with boils and warts.
His grey beard stinks with goat-shit, sweat, and coal.
20   Fire and heated dust have rawed his eyes to redness;
They hit like iron bullets in my guts.
No kindness in him: the long whip smashes on the donkey like on iron.
The black and brittle coal has clogged his chest with dirt,
The black fragrance of the coal is killing him.

25   He is useful still. I shake with pain to see him pass.
He has not lost his hating yet, there's that sweet thing to say,
He farts at the beauty of the raindipped moon.
The smooth men in their livery of success
He curses in his killing heart
30   And yearns for thorns to tear their ease.
His spit blazes in the sun. An emperor's bracelet shines.

PORKNOCKER
Mark McWatt

His fingers felt
along every neck of stone
for a vein of the mountain
until it convulsed in his hand
5   like the pulse of his desire
with sudden, secret data
to his brain.

He jotted on a pad
the longevity and attitude of stone;
10   figures he was certain to forget
in his eruption out of himself
and into his life of gold.

He stood beside himself
when the earth heaved
15   and re-hollowed. Rooted
to granite pirouettes,
the branched
        lightning
of his
20   limbs
       through space
held him prisoner
to the metamorphic rituals of stone;

his tethered soul snapped
25   free, and he knew
like every far flung shard
of the rock's memory:

The cold basaltic pulse
booms once a lifetime
30   and then subsides like a bat's cry
into the depths of earth veins;
the golden net of nerves
with dying hum becomes
again unfeeling—ore of the
porknocker,
35   bauble of a millennium.

And his brain,
indifferent fossil of desire
found ruined among river rocks,
an archeologist's dream
40   like the yellowed map of history
he could never read,
or like the intimations of eldorado
that perished—or were fresh
conceived—
within the dancing seam.

VIRGO
Dawad Phillip

12 years after the selling of her sewing machine
to A M Querino, the town's auctioneer
& her departure from the island
& her enrollment at the Wilfred Academy of
5 Hair Beauty & Culture

12 years since
—in a class of 42 girls all
white
against
10 "I one"—
Virgo topped them all

(You may have read when Eartha Commissiong wrote
in The Talk of Trinidad
saying how
15 "Yuh gyul excelled"
taking three out of five honours
that graduation)

Virgo saying that it was no big thing—
having been a product of the Gibbs School
20 of Beauty & Culture back in Port of Spain
explaining that,
pound for pound, Gibbs could match anything
Wilfred could offer only that
Port of Spain wasn't New York.

25 Today
decorative
two feathers displayed from her red wig
on Fulton Street, Sunday morning
drinking beer from a paper bag
30 tongue like aloes with bitterness
recalling the years & especially nowadays
when even Papa, once a lover dearly devoted
now hides when she passes by his barber shop

Today
35 she warns him that if he did not come out
    now she would
    "Strip every piece ah clothes & stan' up
    outside" until he decided to
    come talk his mind to her face
40 undressing
    & Screaming
    "Papa, Dis is Virgo, y'know. Mister no-teeth,
    don't play wid me. If nobody never tell you
    who you playin' with
45 well run quick an' ask Eartha Commissiong.
    I is somebody, Papa.
    Treat me like somebody."

SWEET MANGO
Andrew Salkey

    Away, here I am,
    in search of a country,
    trying hard to find myself
    a land of fruit trees
5   to return to,
    a sweet mango, perhaps
    with my mother's face
    on its slowly yellowing skin,
    my father's own exile.
10 scattered among the leaves,
    my brother's immaturity
    and my own
    nervously leaping
    up and down
15 on the stones and trash
    which hide the roots
    from all of us.

4
One Love

: for Joy
Dennis Scott

After all journeys, you. And in the centre
of a town where no one had invented trees
yet, I remember
a great kite stumbled
5 like some bird, sun-blind.
The houses spread out their sharp arms
the soiled windows shocked open
the boardings cried out, the walls
sliced cold at the air with their edges
10 till it swung singing at last
aloft into the wind.
And the children floated
against that crooked street
silent as flowers.
15 So, constant, twine me
home through waste, through wind
or hold me high—
I will sing simple as a child's toy, flying
my bones like bamboo
20 at your sky.

DIALOGUE BETWEEN TWO LARGE VILLAGE WOMEN
James Berry

Vergie mi gal, yu know
wha overtek me?

    Wha, Bet-Bet darlin?

Yu know de downgrow bwoy
5 dey call Runt?

    Everybody know de lickle
    forceripe wretch.

Well mi dear, de bwoy put
question to mi?

10   Wha? Wha yu sey?

Yeahs—put question to mi
big-big woman, who could be
him mummah over and over.

15   Laad above. Didn yu bounce
    de damn lickle ramgoat face?

Mi hol him an mi shake
de lickle beas like
to kill de wretch.
An yu know wha happn?

20   No.

De lickle brute try fi kiss mi.

MOMENTS
Robert Lee

Nothing depresses so much as when, caught
Suddenly unawares, the heart and memory

Come face to face and find forgotten pain
In a remembered glance or touch that sought

5 To ease that very hurt. And when, in vain
Later, one tries to fill some emptiness

With some moment that the heart should leave to
Memory, nothing depresses so much.

FOR A SON
Mervyn Morris

Watching you swell
your mother's womb, only a crude
connection seemed to make itself.
Watching your mother swell, with having you,
5 taught tenderness, for she
while growing you was all my care,
happy as she rounded.
Even alive and howling clear
you seemed a thing your mother had.

10 But you yourself I learnt
could make me feel—maybe your laugh,
that warm primordial gurgle, did it:
your personal self enjoined my love,
trying our lives as with the living cord.

15 Be strong my bond and my release
from time. Be tall, stretch separate: and know
the love you've nourished, though you may not care.

BARRIAT
Wordsworth McAndrew

Om shri ganesh, aya nama . . .

To the observer from a different race
the coloured squares of rice hyponotize,
like a face which looks knowing
5   while showing no recognition.
The rice is dyed for symbols—
       blue
       ochre
       white
10   and red,
       bloodred, for life and passion
       like the red ixorias
       suspended over the heads of the holy pair
       who will this moment leap
15   deep into the conjugal estate . . .

       I
       bow
       to thee, O God . . .
the pandit soliloquizes from the north.
20   His words flow forth
         freely
       on the North-East trade wind
while the flame burns steady in the bowl of ghee,
lighting the way to glory of one who is crowned
25   today
       to be king of everything
including a wife he has never seen
whose lips he has never kissed
whose bare black hair and painted toes
30   cry out loud for freedom
from the all-encompassing shroud of white—
       wedding white, for virginity . . .
      . . . Om
        it will not be long now
35   . . . shri
       before they tie
      . . . ganesh

        the magic umbilical of white and pink garments
. . . aya nama
40   it is finished. Henceforth,
these four footsteps shall be one
as the king rises with his handmaid and leads her, veiled,
across the threshold . . .
Under the bamboo where they sat
45   the lahwa smoulders near the tillak
and bares its heart to the wind in a last, loving memory
        of the kangan and the thalee
        and maaroe and nechhu and khichree
        and the badie and paaw poojay
50   the burning dough and wafers thrown over the shoulder
        gifts of notes and silver
        symbols of rice, sugar and flour
          and coconut
and the nibbled holiness of green mango leaves
55   the flowers
the hours of abstinence and preparation. . . .

        Symbols
never before understood by two young Hindus
tumble madly into place around them
60   like a vocalist picking up the tune of a bhajan
        as the plectrum plucks
        coloured squares
        of melody
on the living metal of sitar strings . . .
65   Om
        shri ganesh, aya nama . . .
        I bow to thee, O God . . .
        I
        bow
70   to
        thee.

DECORATED FOR A KISS
Ian McDonald

I come to her house for love with a basket of red petals.
Men-friend tell me what a fool to go to the girl
Come, man, come fish shark, strong white shark,
At midnight come fish golden snapper along the warm black rocks.
5 But I decide my mind and come to her for love.
Her dress is patterned with blue dragon-flies
She has put a red bead in each ear
Green lizards run in her eyes
Her body has the scent of sun-dried khus-khus grass
10 The sweet fibres she has put between the linen since midday
She has washed her mouth with milk
She has rubbed her lips with bay leaves
She has made her limbs clean with water from a green calabash
Now she offers me a few plums and palm-wine from a gourd of scarlet leather.

WIND AND RIVER
ROMANCE
John Agard

Wind forever playing loverboy
bringing he breeze joy
to everything he touch
but Wind you can't trust

5 Forever playing fresh
with big woman like me
He forget I name River—
passing he hand over me face
tickling me bellyskin
10 talking to me in whisper

Promising to bring down
the moon and the stars
and lay them in me lap
even when hot sun shining
15 but sweet whispering don't catch me

I know Wind too good
I does just flow along to faithful Sea
and let Wind sweet words pass by
like cool breeze

WASTING TIME
Opal Palmer

Nooo!
me nah call him
maybe me should?
no sah!
5   mek him guh tink me
a court him.

Cho!
but me would a like
fi call him.
10 but him a guh tink
me a run him down.

No sah!
mek him galang.

But cho!
15 wha it matta
wha him tink.
Me nah run him down.
so might as cheap me call
him.

20 Cho!
dem yah man wan
oman call call dem.
den dem tun roun
tek vantage.
25 but wha me care
dem tek vantage anyway.

Cho!
me nah call him.
maybe me should?
30 No sah!
me nah call nuh man
fi him come breathe
hot air pon me chest
den tun round
35 tek vantage.

but me should a
call him yuh know.

but tap! why him
kyaan call tu.

40 Cho!
a wonda
should me call him though?

(silence, silence, silence)

howdy do man.

45 (hesitation, hesitation,
                hesitation)
I would like fi
speak to
(pause, pause, pause)

I would like fi
50 speak to Missa . . .

FOR MY MOTHER
(MAY I INHERIT HALF HER STRENGTH)
Lorna Goodison

my mother loved my father
I write this as an absolute
in this my thirtieth year
the year to discard absolutes

5 he appeared, her fate disguised,
as a sunday player in a cricket match,
he had ridden from a country
one hundred miles south of hers.

She tells me he dressed the part,
10 visiting dandy, maroon blazer
cream serge pants, seam like razor,
and the beret and the two-tone shoes.

My father stopped to speak to her sister,
till he looked and saw her by the oleander,
15 sure in the kingdom of my blue-eyed grandmother.
He never played the cricket match that day.

He wooed her with words and he won her.
He had nothing but words to woo her,
On a visit to distant Kingston he wrote,

20 "I stood on the corner of King Street and looked,
and not one woman in that town was lovely as you".

My mother was a child of the petit bourgeoisie
studying to be a teacher, she oiled her hands
to hold pens.
25 My father barely knew his father, his mother died
young,
he was a boy who grew with his granny.

My mother's trousseau came by steamer through the
snows of Montreal
30 where her sister Albertha of the cheekbones and the
perennial Rose, combed Jewlit backstreets with French-
turned names for Doris' wedding things.

Such a wedding Harvey River, Hanover, had never seen
Who anywhere had seen a veil fifteen chantilly yards
35   long?
and a crepe de chine dress with inlets of silk godettes
and a neck-line clasped with jewelled pins!

And on her wedding day she wept. For it was a brazen
    bride in those days
40   who smiled.

And her bouquet looked for the world like a sheaf of
    wheat
against the unknown of her belly,
a sheaf of wheat backed by maidenhair fern, represent-
45   ing Harvey River
her face washed by something other than river water.

My father made one assertive move, he took the
    imported cherub down
from the height of the cake and dropped it in the soft
50   territory
between her breasts . . . and she cried.

When I came to know my mother many years later,
    I knew her as the figure
who sat at the first thing I learned to read: "SINGER",
55   and she breast-fed
my brother while she sewed; and she taught us to read
    while she sewed and
she sat in judgement over all our disputes as she sewed.

She could work miracles, she would make a garment
60   from a square of cloth
in a span that defied time. Or feed twenty people on a
    stew made from
fallen-from-the-head cabbage leaves and a carrot and a
    cho-cho and a palmful
65   of meat.

And she rose early and sent us clean into the world
    and she went to bed in
the dark, for my father came in always last.

There is a place somewhere where my mother never
70   took the younger ones
a country where my father with the always smile

my father whom all women loved, who had the
    perpetual quality of wonder
given only to a child . . . hurt his bride.

75 Even at his death there was this "Friend" who stood
    by her side,
but my mother is adamant that that has no place in
    the memory of
my father.

80 When he died, she sewed dark dresses for the women
    among us
and she summoned that walk, straight-backed, that she
    gave to us
and buried him dry-eyed.

85 Just that morning, weeks after
she stood delivering bananas from their skin
singing in that flat hill country voice

she fell down a note to the realization that she did
not have to be brave, just this once
90 and she cried.

For her hands grown coarse with raising nine children
for her body for twenty years permanently fat
for the time she pawned her machine for my sister's
Senior Cambridge fees
95 and for the pain she bore with the eyes of a queen

and she cried also because she loved him.

FAMILY PICTURES
Mervyn Morris

In spite of love
desire to be alone
haunts him like prophecy.

Observe: the baby chuckles,
5 gurgles his delight
that daddy-man is handy,
to be stared at, clawed at,
spitted-up upon;
the baby's elder brother
10 laughs, or hugs, and nags
for popcorn or a pencil
or a trip.

And see: the frazzled wife
who jealously
15 protects the idol infant
from the smallest chance
of harm, and anxious
in the middle of the night
wakes up to coughs; and checks,
20 and loves, and screams
her nerves; but loves him
patient still: the wife
who sweets the bigger boy
and teases him through homework,
25 bright as play.

But you may not observe
(it is a private sanctuary)
the steady glowing power
that makes a man feel loved,
30 feel needed, all of time;
yet frees him, king of her
emotions, jockey of her
flesh, to cherish
his own corner
35 of the cage.

In spite of love
this dream:
to go alone
to where
40 the fishing boats are empty
on the beach
and no one knows
which man is
father, husband, victim,
45 king, the master of one cage.

NURSE GUYADEEN
AND THE PREACHER
Ian McDonald

Best nurse in here was Sati Guyadeen
Bright, loving, strict, humorous and clean.
Dealt briskly with every single chore
Yet strove beyond "Accept, endure,"
5 Sati Guyadeen, fresh morning breeze,
Stepping in on edge of dance,
You made a difference in this place.
Who claims even half-perfection?
Hope and bravery in every glance
10 You nudged life in the right direction.

Big feud broke out once in here:
It livened up the Ward a while.
They brought in Herman Forrester
A pavement-preacher all his life.
15 He had his pitch in Water Street:
Up and down the pave all day,
"Save your soul: Repent, repent!
The world it end tonight at eight,
Repent, repent! It not too late!"
20 Every Friday eleven o'clock
He took his stand by Royal Bank:
"Money is the root of all evil,
It eat out your soul like biscuit-weevil!"
And Wednesday by J P Santos store
25 He lectured on Mosaic law.

In here he didn't stop for breath
All day you heard his preacher-mouth:
"Repent your sins before you die!"
If you were God's children, then all right:
30 He pointed straight up in the sky.
But when he said where sinners go
He pointed dramatically low
Implying that those he saw around
Would taste hell-fire underground.

35   In all the Ward distress began:
    They frighten of this preacher man.
    Who with, say, a month to go
    Likes to be condemned below?

    Nurse Guyadeen, brisk and firm,
40   Decide herself to handle him.
    "People can't have peace in here?
    Hush up, or water pour on you!"
    (She would have poured a drop or two).
    The big feud start up straight away:
45   Preacher-man forget to preach,
    He have a new thing now to do:
    Bad-talking Guyadeen black and blue.
    "Parrot-monkey, La Penitence rat,
    Guyadeen more ugly than that!"
50   He spends his hours thinking hard
    And looking happy when he could shout
    "Someone smell like pit-latrine
    It must have to be Nurse Guyadeen!"
    And Guyadeen giving as good as got
55   Lip match lip, hot for hot
    And when she thinks he gets too fas'
    She jam an enema up his arse.
    The quarrel kept the whole Ward bright:
    Who win today was the talk tonight.
60   For a good ten days they had it out
    Row for row, shout for shout,
    But I noticed how she took her cue:
    He began to weaken, she weakened too.
    The last few days it didn't count
65   His mind wandered North and South
    Sweet Jesus walked in Stabroek Market
    And hóney rained on Zion's Mount.
    "Good riddance!" claimed nurse Guyadeen
    When she came to hear he died at noon;
70   Set straight about her many tasks,
    Brought clean sheets, plumped up the pillows.
    The empty bed was fill by six,
    The new chart written up and fixed.
    She made sure the night-lamps all were lit
75   And then she cried a little bit.

ONE WOMAN
Shake Keane

". . . for me
it only have *one* Woman
in this world
    you hear

5 It must be have
donkey thousand kind o' man
but only one Woman for me

It have   —yo know me father a'ready—
    lemme see
10   boat-man   goat-man
      flirty-man   dutty-man
       seine-man   cane-man   brain-man
      politician

Man
15   all kind o' man
          you hear
  hen-man   fren-man   pen-man
    gun-man
      done-an'-run-man
20   woman

All kind
But only ONE ONE WOMAN

And da's *my mudder*
A true Yellow Woman-Carib
25 And only death could kill she

        So you best hads
        DON'T EVEN CALL SHE NAME . . .

5
Home— City Life

LETTER TO ENGLAND
Fred d'Aguiar

Your letters and parcels take longer
And longer to reach us. The authorities
Tamper with them (whoever reads this
And shouldn't I hope jumbie spit
5   In dem eye). We are more and more
Like another South American dictatorship
And less and less a part of the Caribbean.
Now that we import rice (rice that used
To grow wild!), we queue for most things:
10   Flour, milk, sugar, barley, and fruits
You can't pick anymore. I join them
At 5 a.m. for 9-o'clock opening time,
People are stabbing one another for a place
And half the queue goes home empty handed
15   With money that means next to nothing.
Every meal is salt-fish these days; we even
Curry it! Send a box soon. Pack the basics:
Flour, for some roti, powdered milk
And any news of what's going on here;
20   No luxuries please, people only talk, shoes
Can wait till things improve (dey bound
Fe improve cause dem cawn get no worse!)
Everybody fed-up in truth; since independence
This country hasn't stopped stepping back;
25   And if you leave you lose your birthright:
With all the talk of nationality we still hungry.
Neil has joined the forces against all advice.
He brings home sardines saved from his rations
For our Sunday meal. He wears the best boots
30   In the town. The fair is full of prizes
We threw out in better days and everyone wins
Coconuts. I wouldn't wish this on anyone
But its worse somehow without you here.
Write! We feast on your letters, really.

"Mi C-YaaN beLieVe iT"
Michael Smith

Mi seh mi cyaan believe it
Mi seh mi cyaan believe it
room dem a rent
mi apply widin
5   but as mi go in
cockroach rat an scorpion also come in

waan good
nose haffi run
but me naw go siddung pan igh wall
10   like Humpty Dumpty
mi a face me reality

one lickle bwoy come blow im orn
an mi look pan im wid scorn
an mi realize ow me five bwoy pickney
15   was a victim of de tricks
dem call partisan pally-trix

an mi ban mi belly
an mi bawl
an mi ban mi belly
20   an mi bawl
lawd
mi cyaan believe it
mi seh mi cyaan believe it

Mi daughter bwoyfren name is Sailor
25   an im pass through de port like a ship
more gran pickney fi feed
but de whole a we in need

what a night what a plight
an we cyaan get a bite
30   me life is a stiff fight
an mi cyan believe it
mi seh mi cyaan believe it

Sittin on de corner wid mi fren
talkin bout tings an time
35 mi hear one voice seh
"Who dat?"
Mi seh "A who dat?"
"A who dat a seh who dat
when mi a seh who dat?"

40 When yuh tek a stock
dem lick we dung flat
teet start fly
an big man start cry
an mi cyaan believe it
45 mi seh mi cyaan believe it

De odder day me pass one yard
pan de hill
When mi teck a stock
mi hear "Hey bwoy!"
50 "Yes, Mam?" "Hey bwoy!"
"Yes, Mam?" "Yuh clean up de dawg shit?"
"Yes, Mam"
An mi cyaan believe it
mi seh mi cyaan believe it

55 Doris a modder of four
get a wuk as a domestic
boss man move een
an bap si kaisico she pregnant again
bap si kaisico she pregnant again
60 an mi cyann believe it

Dah yard de odder night
when mi hear "Fire!"
"Fire, to plate claat!"
Who dead? You dead?
65 Who dead? Me dead?
Who dead? Harry dead?
Who dead? Eleven dead
Wooeeeeeeee
Orange Street fire deh pan me head
70 an mi cyaan believe it
mi seh mi cyaan believe it

Lawd, mi see some black bud
livin inna one buildin
but no rent no pay
75   so dem cyaan stay
Lawd, de oppress an de dispossess
cyaan get no res
What nex?

Teck a trip from Kingston
80   to Jamaica
Teck twelve from a dozen
an mi see mi Muma in heaven
MAD OUSE! MAD OUSE!
mi seh mi cyaan believe it
85   mi seh mi cyaan believe it

Yuh believe it?
How yuh fi believe it
when yuh laugh
yuh blind yuh eye to it?
90   But me know yuh believe it
mi know yuh believe it . . .

NO MAN'S LAND
Gloria Escoffery

The body of a fourteen year old playing politics
Makes a hummock on the ground beside his ratchet knife
Which drew blood but cannot bleed for him.
The muzzle of a sawn-off shot gun masks the eye of one
5   Who, being a man (?), thinks himself a great gun.
The gully scrub cannot hide him forever:
Silenced, he drops the gun and becomes a dead man.

Now the killer's "baby mother" is caught by the press photographer;
For the morning paper and forever she throws up her arms
10   In the traditional gesture of prayer.
Wai oh! Aie! Eheu! mourns the camera shot matron
Whose stringy son, like a sucked mango seed,
Lies there no more use to anyone;
Soon to be inseparable from the rest of the levelled ground.
15   Why this pieta needs to be enacted in our land
No one can explain:
It clearly belongs within the pieties of a museum frame.
Is there no way but through this scene?

A SLUM DWELLER DECLARES
Oku Onuora

wi wan
fi free
free from misery
wi wan
5 fi live
like humanbeing
wi nu mean
fi live
pon dump
10 mongs
dead dawg
an fly
an haffi a fight
johncrow from sky
15 fi get food fi nyam
wi waan
fi live
like any adda man
yu believe wi com ya willinly?
20 yu believe wi waan
wi pickney dem fi grow up
inna place worse dan hag pen?
wi waan
fi live
25 like humanbeing. . . .

TRENCH TOWN SHOCK (A SOH DEM SEY)
Valerie Bloom

Waia, Miss May, trouble dey yah,
Ban yuh belly, Missis, do.
Mi ha' one terrible piece o' news,
An mi sarry fe sey it consarn yuh.

5 Yuh know yuh secon' or t'ird cousin?
Yuh great-aunt Edith Fred?
Im pick up imse'f gawn a pickcha show
An police shot im dead.

But a di bwoy own fault yah mah,
10 For im go out o' im way
Fi gawn fas' wid police-man,
At leas' a soh dem sey.

Dem sey im a creep oba di teata fence,
Dem halla "who go deh?"
15 De bwoy dis chap one bad wud mah,
At leas' a soh dem sey.

De police sey "tap or we opin fiah".
But yuh know ow di bwoy stay,
Im gallop back come attack dem,
20 At leas' a soh dem sey.

Still, nutten woulda come from i',
But what yuh tink, Miss May?
Di bwoy no pull out lang knife mah!
At leas' a soh dem sey.

25 Dem try fi aim afta im foot
But im head get een di way,
Di bullit go 'traight through im brain,
At leas' a soh dem sey.

Dry yuh yeye, mah, mi know i hat,
30 But i happen ebery day,
Knife-man always attack armed police
At leas' a soh dem sey.

RED HILLS
Wayne Brown

Hyphen-stretched, between Mustang and mule,
the road trundles its garbage.
Who'd have thought love was so precise?

We arrive, sweating
5   from the long climb up,
loosen our ties and lapse

into grins. Red hillscar, red
nigger preserve,
our roses bloom whitely here.

10   The instamatic transfiguring glare
of T.V. sunsets, Alsatians.

Each evening, each streetlamp long,
fumbling with padlocks, we keep love in
and find no use for memory, though

15   the figure in the garden,
lost in weed,
bloom towards us with red eyes,

and the unmentionable dog
limps moonward like Santa,
20   a hole in its head,

dragging its bone.

Ad. FOR A
HOUSING SCHEME
Anthony McNeill

Packed tightly like
sums. Their sheer
geometrical lines oppress
architecturally, appearing
5   disinterested, loveless, same.

People who drive past these houses
see them as stacked
-up z—
ros to be quickly got through;
10 accelerate, almost
by instinct, to have them
behind their tail pipe
like bad dreams or carcases.

Mine, positioned
15 in from the highway, assails
few sensitive motorists, but I,
walking toward its box-
shape this twilight,
see it as part
20 of a huge, grotesque tenement: my house
is ugly for being anonymous.

And now suddenly
the grey, uniform buildings
intersect like years. Poised
25 only for home, I cross
into a harsh, formularized future
where houses and people
flash smally and strictly alike.

FEWCHA GAAN
Fred Nunes

Six a we!
      in a daak muddy likkle
            'ole;
bang-belly nose naught
5   sore-foot
an' 'ungry pickney bawlin'.

All a we!
      stuff-up stuff-up
          in a dim san' dash
10   bax:
bruk slate tight skirt
            tear pants
an' tick strap comin dung de line.

Houtside!
15   sunshine
breeze an' trees an' sea.
          An' woman
big-belly uman.
          No wok
20   Troubles.

A fe me!
      pickney 'ungry mus' get
        food.
              Gimme!
25 Stone and knife and gun.
Moneyman run.
          Babylon come.

Me alone!
      lock up tight
30 eena cole stone cell.
Lashin'
         man-love
           blood—
what a way dem teach.

35 It is I!
        Ras Tafari—
        No wok.
Frens inside in cell—
some gaan   some dead
40 Ship come   ship sink   'ope gaan.

40 lunch and tea
                    While with a forward defensive
                    assertive prod,
                    stroking the "beef" from the valley
    Continually-moving meh back-side
45 more squarer to the off side
    near a gully
                    Dividing hours
                    into butt-ends, or romy
                                    hands
50   or marking race
                                    programmes.
    Now an then
    as Mighty Suck Eye,
    serenading some tourists—
55   hustling some coins
                                for a
                                four-tirty
    Lolling in a snackette
                    bush-rum quelling the pain
60   in meh guts
    While the Redding
    sitting on the dock.
                    Staring at the "No Hands
                                Wanted" signs
65   The National Lottery Sold
                                Here signs
                    and the long line——
                    The lime near Marli Street.
    Pulling at meh weed
70 Smoking out meh need
    Cursing dem all
    Forgetting it all
                            Swaying down the kiss meh
                                            arse
75   streets
                            to a rhythm rehearsed in bed
                            and the down beat in meh
                                            head
    And over head the sun strumming along,
80 lashing along meh back,
    and I calling dat George
    substituting half measures

    for the w-hole.

DOWN BEAT
Victor D Questel

A pocket
   myself an arse
a stick of grass
Pinching all to stay alive.

5   Head line   a sports page
                  Hem-lines   a body line
                  Glancing, heckling: all the
                                time
                  Leaning on Ma Dolly fence

10   Waiting for time to pass
            for the mark to buss
            for the chance
            to ask Chin for trus'.
                        Into Town
15   dark-glasses-glass-cases—
                  staring at faces
                      staring-listening-moving
                Down-Town.
Welcoming Snake Eye
20   Out from jail
with a fete,
                sparing a hasty regret
                for the ting
                he rape
25   While remembering last night wake;
Working on meh sweet mas',
Clanging iron when Carnival in season,
                For no reason
                following some demon-
30   stration
Tuning in on the latest rake
or crash programme
Waiting for the next election.
                Talking cricket-talk
35   Jiving on a side walk
                Talking ol'-talk
Like say
how many Left-Overs
between tea

LAVENTILLE
Derek Walcott

(for V S Naipaul)

To find the Western Path
Through the Gates of Wrath
BLAKE

It huddled there
steel tinkling its blue painted metal air,
tempered in violence, like Rio's favelas,

with snaking, perilous streets whose edges fell as
5   its episcopal turkey-buzzards fall
from its miraculous hilltop

shrine,
down the impossible drop
to Belmont, Woodbrook, Maraval, St Clair

10   that shine
like peddlers' tin trinkets in the sun.
From a harsh

shower, its gutters growled and gargled wash
past the Youth Centre, past the water catchment,
15   a rigid children's carousel of cement;

we climbed where lank electric
lines and tension cables linked its raw brick
hovels like a complex feud,

where the inheritors of the middle passage stewed
20   five to a room, still clamped below their hatch,
breeding like felonies,

whose lives revolve round prison, graveyard, church.
Below bent breadfruit trees
in the flat, coloured city, class

25   lay escalated into structures still,
merchant, middleman, magistrate, knight. To go downhill
from here was to ascend.

The middle passage never guessed its end.
This is the height of poverty
30   for the desperate and black;

climbing, we could look back
with widening memory
on the hot, corrugated iron sea
whose horrors we all

35   shared. The salt blood knew it well,
you, me, Samuel's daughter, Samuel,
and those ancestors clamped below its grate.

And climbing steeply past the wild
gutters, it shrilled
40   in the blood, for those who suffered, who were killed,

and who survive.
What other gift was there to give
as the godparents of his unnamed child?

Yet outside the brown annexe of the church, the
45   stifling odour of bay rum and talc, the particular,
neat sweetness of the crowd distressed

that sense. The black, fawning verger
his bow tie akimbo, grinning, the clown-gloved
fashionable wear of those I deeply loved

50   once, made me look on with hopelessness and rage
at their new, apish habits, their excess
and fear, the possessed, the self-possessed;

their perfume shrivelled to a childhood fear
of Sabbath graveyards, christenings, marriages,
55   that muggy, steaming, self-assuring air

of tropical Sabbath afternoons. And in
the church, eyes prickling with rage,
the children rescued from original sin

by their God-father since the middle passage,
60   the supercilious brown curate, who intones,

healing the guilt in these rachitic bones,
twisting my love within me like a knife,
"across the troubled waters of this life . . ."

Which of us cares to walk
65   even if God wished
those retching waters where our souls were fished

for this new world? Afterwards, we talk
in whispers, close to death
among those stones planted on alien earth.

70 Afterwards,
  the ceremony, the careful photograph
  moved out of range before the patient tombs,

  we dare a laugh,
  ritual, desperate words,
75 born like these children from habitual wombs,

  from lives fixed in the unalterable groove
  of grinding poverty. I stand out on a balcony
  and watch the sun pave its flat, golden path

  across the roofs, the aerials, cranes, the tops
80 of fruit trees crawling downward to the city.
  Something inside is laid wide like a wound,

  some open passage that has cleft the brain,
  some deep, amnesiac blow. We left
  somewhere a life we never found,

85 customs and gods that are not born again,
  some crib, some grill of light
  clanged shut on us in bondage, and withheld

  us from that world below us and beyond,
  and in its swaddling cerements we're still bound.

SONNET TO NEW FLOWERS
Mahadai Das

  In the rectangular and tall absence
  Of the builder's art, wrecked tenements stand,
  Bricknude, aggressively branded against
  lewd lack of tree, flower or friendly hand.
5 Windows with broken glass stare, token
  gazes sent from iron-fisted buildings.
  In desolate air, indifferent haze,
  Hate stares in gunshot-interrupted
  Silence. Black flowers materialise late
10 from the dark, wounds in their sides.
  Here, in this arena of smoking eyes,
  dope, and hounds among poor-inhabited
  tenements, hope, absent watercan, has
  never lent itself to flowers.

SUNDAY CROSSES
Jean Goulbourne

The rastaman
came
to the door
that Sunday
5   and said
"Broom"

Sun overhead
as hot as hell
gate burnt brown
10   grass grey
under violent
Sunday Sun—
Head wrapped
with cotton closet
15   of lice and worms—
Death squawking at squaw
and children
nimbling worms—
bellies banged
20   when hunger
clanged its bell—

Rastaman stopped
at brown
sun baked door
25   and said
"Broom".

Door opened Hope
and brown skinned man
with curly hair

30   a bank account
and good solid credit
at every bank
in town,
poked head out
35   wrinkled nose
at sweaty sun
day smell
and said

"No broom"

40   Door closed doom
and sun went out
like a light
grass grew greyer
dark clouds bleaker
45   man looked at speaker
at the blank mass
of a brown skinned
uncaring futile face
and sighs.

50   Proud man
pickney down gutter
waiting
commonlaw wife
breeding
55   son succeeding
at nothing—
moves slowly cross
concrete
on a Sunday full
60   of crosses
and calls
"Broom".

6
*Home—
Country Life*

THE DUST
Edward Kamau Brathwaite

Evenin' Miss
Evvy, Miss
Maisie, Miss
Maud. Olive,

5 how you? How
you, Eveie, chile?
You tek dat Miraculous Bush
fuh de trouble you tell me about?

Hush!
10 Doan keep so much noise
in de white people shop!

But you tek
it?

Ev'ry night 'fore uh gets
15 into bed.

Uh bet-
'cha you feelin' less
poorly a'ready!

I int know, Pearlie,
20 man. Any-
way, the body int dead.

No man, you even lookin'
more hearty!

A'ready?
25 Then all uh kin say
an' uh say it agen:
we got to thank God
fuh small mercies.

Amen,
30 Eveie, chile.
Amen,
Eveie, chile

an' agen
I say is Amen.

35 Miss Evvy, uh wants
you to trus' me half
pung-a-flour an'two
cake o' soap till
Mundee come wid de will
40 o' de Lord.

Write two
cake o' soap an' half
pung-a flour in Olive black balance
book fuh me, Maisie muh dear.
45 An' Olive—

doan fuhget 'bout de
biscuit an' sawlfish
you daughter Marilyn
come here an' say that you wish
50 to tek out las' month!
Mundee Dee Vee, uh settlin'
up ev'ry brass bill an' pen-
ny that owin' this shop, Miss
Olive muh dear.

55 Hey Mary!
You there?
I int see you there
wid you head half hide
in de dark o' dat crocus bag. How
60 Darrington mule?

He still sicky-sicky. An' now
I hear dat de cow
gone down too. It int give no milk
since las' Tuesdee.

65 Is de pes-
tilence, man.
Same kind o' sickness,
like wickedness, man, dis-
favour de yams.

70 Is true. Bolinjay,
spinach, wither-face cabbage,
muh Caroline Lee an' the Six Weeks,
too;
greens swibble up an' the little blue
leafs o' de Red Rock slips
getting' dry
75 dry dry.

Is de pes-
tilence, man.
Mister Gilkes say is a test
o' de times like the nine-
80 teen fourteen an' eighteen
war when they burn out 'e balls
wid dat yellowin' mustard gas.

An' if you as'
me, there soon goin'
85 to be fresh wars an' rumours
of wars.

But is
true.

Is
90 the pes-
tilence, man. You
int hear
the silence? Pastor
say las' night in the Chapel
95 that the Writin' Han' pun the Wall.

But that isn't all!
you remember that story
Gran' tell us 'bout May
dust?

100 No! What nother fuss
that?

Well it seem that
they have a mountain near hey
that always smokin' an' boilin'
105 like when you belly got bile.

What you sayin', chile!

But is
true

Now how you
110 know! Any-
body live there? You
know any-
body from there who
live out near here?
115 Besides, where
exactly you say this place is?

That isn't you biz-
ness! Besides,
is miles an' miles
120 from the peace o' this

place an' is
always purrin' an' pourin'
out smoke. Some say
is in one o' them islands away
125 where they language tie-tongue
an' to hear them speak so
in they St Lucia patois
is as if they cahn unnerstan'

a single word o' English.
130 But uh doan really know. All uh know
is that one day suddenly so
this mountain leggo one *brugg-a-lung-go*

whole bloody back side
o' this hill like it blow
135 off like they blastin' stones
in the quarry.

Rocks big as you cow pen hois'
in the air as if they was one
set o' shingles. That noise,
140 Jesus Christ, mussa rain down

splinter an' spark
as if it was Con-
federation.

But you int got to call
145   the Lord name in vain
to make we swallow
this tale! It int nice,

Olive, man!

It is true!
150   An' the Lord God
know that uh sorry.

But it black black black
from that mountain back:
in yuh face, in yuh food,

155   in yuh eye. In fac',
Granny say, in de broad
day light, even de white

o' she skylight went out.
An' if you hear people shout!
160   how they can't find the way

how they isn't have shelter
can't pray to no priest or no leader
an' God gone an' darken the day!

Gran' say that even the fowls in the yard
165   jump back pun they coops when the air
turn grey an' the cocks start to crow
as if it was foreday mornin'.

It went dark dark dark
as if it was night
170   an' uh fright-
en, you know,

when uh hear things so;
is make me wonder an'
pray: 'cause uh say

175   to meself: Olive, chile,
you does eat an' sleep
an' try to fuhget

some o' de burdens
you back got to bear;
180   you does drink, dance

sometimes pun a Sar'dee
night, meet yuh man
an' if God bless yuh, beget

Yuh does get up, walk 'bout,
185   praise God that yuh body
int turnin' to stone,

an' that you bubbies still big;
that you got a good
voice that can shout

190   for heaven to hear
you: int got nothin' to fear
from no man. You does come

to the shop, stop, talk
little bit, get despatch
195   an' go home;

you still got a back that kin dig
in the fields
an' hoe an' pull up the weeds

from the peeny brown
200   square that you callin' you own;
you int sick an' you children strong;

ev'ry day you see the sun
rise, the sun
set; God sen' ev'ry month

205   a new moon. Dry season
follow wet season again
an' the green crop follow the rain.

An' then suddenly so
widdout rhyme
210   widdout reason

you crops start to die
you can't even see the sun in the sky;
an' suddenly so, without rhyme,

without reason, all you hope gone
215   ev'rything look like it comin' out wrong.
Why is that? What it mean?

THINKING BACK
ON YARD TIME
James Berry

We swim in the mooneye.
The girls brown breasts float.
Sea sways against sandbanks.

We all frogkick water.
5 Palm trees stand there watching
with limbs dark like our crowd.

We porpoise-dive, we rise,
we dog-shake water from our heads.
Somebody swims on somebody.

10 We laugh, we dry ourselves.
Sea-rolling makes thunder
around coast walls of cliffs.

Noise at Square is rum-talk
from the sweaty rum bar
15 without one woman's word.

Skylarking, in our seizure,
in youthful bantering,
we are lost in togetherness.

Our road isn't dark tonight.
20 Trees—mango, breadfruit—all,
only make own shapely shadow.

Moon lights up pastureland.
Cows, jackass, all, graze quietly.
We are the cackling party.

WHEN MOON SHINE
Paul Keens-Douglas

Tim, Tim? . . . papa welcome!
Ah send an' call de doctor
An' de doctor reach before me?
Don't tell me, ah know—coconut!
5   Is Nanci story time on de step,
Is full moon an' everything bright.
All little children teafin' ah "stay up",
Playin' rounders an' catchers,
Nobody mind, not when de moon full,
10   Is like everybody find excuse
To leave de house
Tanti on de porch lookin' out,
"Cover yu head, gal, yu want dew kill yu?"
But Tanti mind elsewhere like she eye.
15   Long time now she watchin' dem two shadow—
Two dat look like one—under de mango tree.
Other tings goin' on beside catchers
    tonite.
Tanti like de moon—she silent, but she see.
20   Two little shadow watchin' de two big
    shadow.
"How we go get de mango with dem dey?
Boy, we must be kill priest, we have cuss?"
Sounds of laughter in de backyard,
25   "High, Low, Jack, Game, yu mudder!
Take dat, I is ah livin 'ground-god.'"
"Pas de bottle an' shut yu mouth!
Dis time is my turn to share.
Evadne—O—O bring some chaser for poopa.
30   Dat little gal bright, yu hear,
All she does study is book an' ting.
Not like he brudder—see him out dere?
He wutless for so—play, dat is he.
Samuel—yu finish yu homework?"
35   "Long time, poopa—ah do it in school!"
"I've got a heavenly sword (Sing)
Teach me to use it well!"
"Ah wish dat damn preacher woman
would stop singin' she hymns,

40   Like de moonlight gone to she head.
     Anne, shell de peas, not eat dem.
     Gal, yu can't do nothin' right?
     An' watch out for dem worms.
     Nite, nite, neighbour, been to church?"
45   "No, me dear, ah been by de market,
     Big political meetin' goin' on,
     Scandal for so, me belly near bus' with laugh.
     Ah leave before me an' Jano come to blows.
     De man stink, stink ah rum,
50   An' come pushin' up in me face,
     An' on top of dat want to hit me.
     Dey had to hold me, ah would ah kill he.
     He must ah tink Jesus bury in my mouth,
     He find out different——ah cuss he in
55   three language."
     "Dats right me dere—dem too ting up
        these days.
     Yu hear 'bout de harvest next month?
     Father say everybody must put up."
60   "Father all right, me dere,
     He an' he church,
     If is not de ole roof to fix
     Is de new one—me gone."
     "Samuel leggo of yu sister
65   Dat is no way to treat a gal,
     Furthermore, pass inside,
     It gettin' late, yu hear me?"
     "Leh we play one last round."
     "Like de preacher woman gone to bed."
70   "Dem two gone, but now Tanti go see we,
     We go fix dem mango tomorrow nite."
     "Nite, nite. neighbour, we go catch up.
     Boy, if dis moon could only talk!". . . .

A SEA-CHANTEY
Derek Walcott

Là, tout n'est qu'ordre et beauté,
Luxe, calme, et volupté.

Anguilla, Adina,
Antigua, Cannelles,
Andreuille, all the l's,
Voyelles, of the liquid Antilles,
5 The names tremble like needles
Of anchored frigates,
Yachts tranquil as lilies,
In ports of calm coral,
The lithe, ebony hulls
10 Of strait-stitching schooners,
The needles of their masts
That thread archipelagoes
Refracted embroidery
In feverish waters
15 Of the sea-farer's islands,
Their shorn, leaning palms,
Shaft of Odysseus,
Cyclopic volcanoes,
Creak their own histories,
20 In the peace of green anchorage;
Flight, and Phyllis,
Returned from the Grenadines,
Names entered this sabbath,
In the port-clerk's register;
25 Their baptismal names,
The sea's liquid letters,
Repos donnez a cils . . .
And their blazing cargoes
Of charcoal and oranges;
30 Quiet, the fury of their ropes.
Daybreak is breaking
On the green chrome water,
The white herons of yachts
Are at sabbath communion,

35 The histories of schooners
Are murmured in coral,
Their cargoes of sponges
On sandspits of islets
Barques white as white salt
40 Of acrid Saint Maarten,
Hulls crusted with barnacles,
Holds foul with great turtles,
Whose ship-boys have seen
The blue heave of Leviathan,
45 A sea-faring, Christian,
And intrepid people.

Now an apprentice washes his cheeks
With salt water and sunlight.

In the middle of the harbour
50 A fish breaks the Sabbath
With a silvery leap.
The scales fall from him
In a tinkle of church-bells;
The town streets are orange
55 With the week-ripened sunlight,
Balanced on the bowsprit
A young sailor is playing
His grandfather's chantey
On a trembling mouth-organ.
60 The music curls, dwindling
Like smoke from blue galleys,
To dissolve near the mountains.

The music uncurls with
The soft vowels of inlets,

65 The christening of vessels,
    The titles of portages,
    The colours of sea-grapes,
    The tartness of sea-almonds,
    The alphabet of church-bells,
70 The peace of white horses,
    The pastures of ports,
    The litany of islands,

    The rosary of archipelagoes,
    Anguilla, Antigua,
75 Virgin of Guadeloupe,
    And stone-white Grenada
    Of sunlight and pigeons,
    The amen of calm waters,
    The amen of calm waters,
80 The amen of calm waters.

THE TOURISTS
Wayne Brown

'The sun works for the Tourist Board'
was a bad joke. But now each noon
the sun toils like a fisherman
with a hard tide to beat,
5   or a farmer whose wife will drop soon.

And in truth the beach is replete
with strangers. Each one arranges
tenderly his limbs for those brass rays
as a woman, testing each pose, changes
10 into nothing for her lover's gaze.

The natives mind their own business.
Some blond types are at it again.
An English anthropologist
praises the texture of a seine.
15 The sea's heard it all before.

A scene from a tourist
brochure. Under that sun
all is languid, and those who come
will find nothing unusual, not
20 one gesture or motion overdone.

But for one parrot fish which turns
grave somersaults on the stainless steel
spear that's just usurped its dim
purpose; which was to swim
25 as usual through blue air, in silence, like the sun.

RICE
Martin Carter

What is rain for, if not rice
for an empty pot; and pot for
in a hungry village? The son
succeeds his father in a line,
5   to count as he did, waiting,
adding the latest to the first
of his losses; his harvests
of quick wind padi. For him
the new moon was dry like the full moon
10   that promised. The sea always
as salt as wet. In his calculation
his yield was the share that he would reap
when he cheated, like the moon and the sea.

AIRY HALL ICONGRAPHY
Fred d'Aguiar

The Tamarind hangs its head,
stings the eyes with its breath.

The Mango traps the sun by degrees,
transforms its ray into ambrosia.

5   The Coconut's perfect seal lets in rain,
bends with solid milk and honey.

The Guava is its own harvest,
each seed bound in fleshy juice.

The Guinep's translucence is all yours
10   if you skin its lips, chew its seed for the raw.

The Stinking-toe might be lopped off a stale foot,
on the tongue it does an about-turn: myrrh.

The Paw-paw runs a feather along your nose,
you want it to stop, you want more.

15   The Sour-sop's veneer is the wasp
treading air at the vaulted honeycomb.

The Sapodilla ducks you twice in frankincense,
you are fished out fighting to go down a third time.

"THE FISHERMEN"
(from SUN POEM)
Edward Kamau Brathwaite

In the great purple dawn the fishermen poured like priests to the
shore. it was dark where they stopped, filling their cans with water
that swished from the pipe like wind through a key hole: the tone
getting deeper as the bucket filled up. then they moved on: walk-
5   ing in twos and in threes: tall black monks of the morning light
wrapped in their cloaks because of the cold and their anti-salt-
water coats; walking out of the night down the street ahead of the sun
and under the leaves of the seagrape and cordia trees whose
flowers were fast fading stars in the touching them softly light.
10   and before the houses awoke, before fathers opened windows and
doors, at the time when the first cocks crowed and the last dogs

barked at the passing ghost (so the housewives said) the fishermen
were away . . . one handed sculling: oar at the back of their black
moses boats: twisting and turning and making an eight in the
15   water still suddenly bright with darkest-night bubbles and break-
outs of light . . . a splash and a voice to a voice across water like a
seine net tossed across silence . . . then the squeak and slide as the
sail-ropes pulled through the pulleys and the brown triangles of
sail went up, catching the wind and the tree-top light as the sky
20   grew bright: mirrors to wind and to light . . . and so the fisher-
mens wakes were wide and away before the houses awoke. each
boat with its three priests huddled and humbled over a prayer:
their steering eyes already miles down the rising horizon . . .

PELTING BEES
Ian McDonald

By July the bees have built in the samans:
There are honey-hives in the notches of those burly trees there.
Today is Sunday. I go out and pelt them with white stones,
And duck quick under the river-bank, my feet in the cold
5   water on the white stones.
How they get up in golden arms then and make a noise
    like breezes!
I hide and watch and again throw white stones with the
    strength of my arm!
10   Nectar-sweet streams from the rich red honeycombs,
The golden bees blaze with fury in the sun.
I laugh and laugh, pelting white stones from the safety of
    Easter river.

IN THE GENTLE AFTERNOON
Royston Ellis

Such commerce
for a small village without a representative
on Central Government, without a village council,
without a working public toilet, with two
5   stand pipes, three rum shops and a cricket pitch;
such business
as citizens sit on benches and discuss
the latest test scores, last night's trouble
at the dance, Sunday's chance in the rounders match
10   the price of cod fish, the problems of cross week;
such activity
late in the afternoon on Friday as mother
rushes over to seize her child; boys plot;
a girl shouts her directions, a jeep coughs
15   to a standstill by the shop, and erupts an eager crowd;
such peace
in the gentle afternoon, as the sun begins to die
and everybody drifts away to attend their affairs
all part of the village family, all private people
20   with each a share of secrets, known by all.

LETTER TO ENGLAND
Bruce St John

Girl chile darling yuh ole muddah hay
Praisin' de Lord fuh 'E blessing an 'E mercies
You is many many blessin's an' all o' me mercies
Glory to God!
5   Uh get de 5 pound note an' de Christmas card
God bless yuh!
But de carpenter ain' come to put on de shed-roof
So uh spen' it an uh sen' Rosy pretty to de
Exhibition gal, yuh should see she!
10   Next month when yuh sen me allowance again,
We will see wuh kin happen in de name i' de Lord.

De Cashmere sweater dat yuh sen' muh so soft
An so warm, uh kin nevah nevah fuget muh
Poor li'l' chile. Sister Reed can'
15   Brag pun me like before, tink she one got
Daughter in England? Uh wear um down to
Service t'ree Sunday mornin' straight an'
Den all bout de place fuh to show dem
I en common, but Lord I haffa tell yuh
20   Dat it ketch 'pon a nail in de kitchen, so,
Bless you love don' f'get to sen' anedduh one,
Uh paint up de place an' varnish de furnitures
An' Lord mek peace dat t'ief charge muh so
High dat I ain't got a cent lef' to brighten
25   Muh face, so de Lord will bless yuh
Don' fo'get you ole muddah, lonely
An' t'ankful, wukkin' she finger to de
Bone, she soul case droppin' out, Wuh law!
I does pray day an' night fuh yuh
30   Come back child, I does cry, I does grieve but

De Lord unde'stand, I closes now
Wid love an' gratitude, care yuhself
Doan le' da man dat yuh married
To upset yuh, le' de Lord
35   An' yuh poor ole muddah keep a
Place in yuh heart. Amen. Amen.

COUNTRY DAYS
Willi Chen

I long for roads claggy and rutted brown
That roll below trundling wheels of bullocks,
The raw bovine heat below my whip.
The grinding, greaseless axle, timeless
5   Spins its groaning passage
Through furrows of shivering cane.

Above, the noonday sky,
Floating corbeaux wheel a circumventing theme,
Stitching cloud on cloud
10   The whisking churr of semps, sissisebs
Echoes the Grassy's gleeful song on stems
Yielding, tilting to the weight of seeds.

Feel the winds replete the song,
The soughing, whispering, rustling tunes
15   Of dry seasons.
Smell the sugar, syrup, all
Sweet fragrance perfumes the air
Dripping brown on cold sleepers, horizontal
To the rumbling roll of cane wagons.

20   Rustic, the mouldering shingles
Verdigris with moss, verge
From sloping walls, the carat
Blazes hot from sunstroke.
Heat flattens the dogs to sleep
25   Under almond shade, a muted mat.

I long for classrooms, dusty, chalk-ridden walls
Ink-stained, pitchpine desk tops
Riddled, niched by scribing nibs
That dip the porcelain pots
30   And cull their meandering infant rhymes.
At recess, before the clangorous bell
Sits us straight, arms folded
Where, mindful of Sybil and Joe—
We pen our frilly frescoes on backsteps,
35   The teachers' encumbering stares on murals
Diminish the crumbling crayons.

Diminishing like palling memory
Like fading nostalgia
The glimpse of tempestuous heaven vanishes
40 Before the storm in the playfields; the rush
Of children barefooted who thud
Their trampling, spattering steps
Across dun-ochre yards, seas of mud.

Then the grasslands.
45 Muted green in a pallette of olive
Fading two tones lower to sienna
Than the rust-ochre blades aglint,
Crowning the coconuts
Lining the twisting road—
50 Incandescent ribbon
In open sunlight.

I hear birds, their mellowing twitter faint;
The quiet murmur of a child's heartbeat
In the crouched shade of bent grass
55 Where the whisk of winds, tremulous
Soothes my breast; the fluttering
Eyelids are stilled and I listen,
Listen for the music of warbling
Robins, their trembling throats honey-toned.

60 And, above me,
The sky stretched like turquoise gauze tighter
Than drumskin.

Disconsolate, in the hot-white swept yard of sand,
Etched by nervous toe prints we marched in penance
65 Around the almond tree. The hollering voices beckoned
Us behind the quivering hedges that ringed,
Ringed our discomfort, our tyranny, while pages
Tore with the wind from our books under rocks
Too light for their purpose. The rage in her eyes.
70 Was sharper than Miss Xavier's ruler curving overhead.
So, we kept on circling until the flame of leaves
Russet-brown cooled. The sun's smothering lantern
Lowered its wick, the teacher's wrath calmed
With the shadows. In other places, life began.

75   Dawn broke the back of a mountain afire
     Lazing its squatting humps ridged on the plain,
     Until scabrous in light holding their spears,
     Plumed in the aura of swathing afterglow,
     The coconuts shook off sleep and whistled the mahoe
80   Sandbox, samaan, the towering crapaud
     Reeked with lichen, chataigne and plantain,
     Roused by the shafts piercing the clouds,
     Until voices, singeing pots sowed a refrain,
     To the chorus of sounds in the lonely country road.

7
Old Folks, Death and Grief

INDIGONE
Edward Kamau Brathwaite

I

Now we is all gathered here at grandfather's hoom in the small
    front room in the house
in the country where the rains
came down and the ponds were big with its photographs of
5   daughters in white organdie:

hands touching gently the artificial vase
of flowers: in white socks: since everything was blackandwhite the
    memory
of cofflewalks and shackles my sister with her teddybear her eyes
10   black liquid dew

drops and technicolour-tinted-behind-glass: joe louee with his
    powderpuff the dionne-
ese quin/triplicates with soap grandfather did not sell the royal
    family
15 in sundaypowderpink a rosicrucian EYE staring from rays of
    cloud that quite trans/
figured me and above the doorway into where we ate CHRIST IS
    THE HEAD OF THIS HOUSE

a gramophone its corrugated trumpet silver handle spinning
20   dog/such faithfulness it
heard it made you sick: *red sails in the sun/set/when the roll* and
    i'll be dead when
you glad you rascal you: okeh and *victor vox trot vox trot vox*
    trot blue bird and *his*
25 *masters vice* the radio that worked on uncle's lorry batteries and
    rocking chairs
of ethiopian lions that ogoun carved and cared for during the
    earth tremor of selassie's

war

30 the window in the little redwood gallery where i'd sit for hours
watching the canefields groan the blackbirds march across the
    road
the sun swing downwards to the shakshak
tree the mulecarts creak/ing home the way
35 the donkey dung was trod and round and burst like pods along
    the golden ground

and nighttime when the crickets became stars
and comets smoked high up among the betujels and jewels of
    orion and the flare of mars
40   the lighthouse distant beyond distance beyond fields
now silvery like nerves in darkness like quixote with his lance of
    light
searching for salt for dead souls for

we were dead: the us/not us: the dust: blood
45   spilled: green branches of the family bone cut off
from root and rib and culture: grand
father dead my father's further genitor
of futures past my borning ancestor

still burning in a room he'd left and still lay in:
50   a window open on his face so we could see and not
see him could recognize and not know him: be
coming *mmmmm*: the candle and the wax and ashes
and the closed cold ingrown ice face of that doll they'd placed in
    there

55   that could not look back out: six feet of him six feet deep down
    already in
the centre of that whirlpool room. we moved around his hool and
    silent howl
and rule and role of darkness: eyeless and leafless, graze/less

60   and we were there/not there the undertaker anxious with his mop
    and kerchief
screw/driver hammer ready for the wrench and damp and
    everlasting itch
but mek e bide a lil bit more aunt evvy said *he int goin down de*
65   *road dis time to soon come back*

and i looked up to see my father's eye: wheeling towards his
    father
now as i his sun moved upward to his eye
brow lifed clear and high above his i
70   trying to fend off the fear he was fearing
the pain that was pealing his head like a bell
the eyewater filling his skull like a shell

that ole rugged cross and that scarecrow

fragments of error/fragments of bone
75   but always that look confident now and un/broken
shattering the rain/blow

II

but suns don't know when they die
      they never give up
      hope heart or articule

80   gases gathered far back before they were born
      before their fathers dived down the shore of the dawn

storing up their megalleons of light
      colliding with each other, hissing their white sperms of
        power
85   and continue to steam, issue heat, long after their tropic
        is over

so that they sweat, fevers of light years away
      though the age freezes over their eye
      though their intemperate i: ron has already wrinkled to
90   rust

and the dead son, ex-
      plosionless socket
      collapses slowly into its shrinks

and the stars, soft watches of night
95   fires of lizards and moths that loved power
      gravitational cool of your arm/pits

      weep tears of light
      for the memories, warmings of ecstasy, head tossed
      in the hollow of pillow they cried out was love

100   while others, more distant, further from that howl and hammer

seek newer longer more elliptical orbits
crabs cassiopeas andromedas
black lidded electronical caves bulg
ing with star-dust

105   but the boy walking the beach of his birth this day does not know
      this
        yet
and there is no one able to tell him this
        yet

110   stepping on bird toes blind eyes of wet feet winning towards his
      love

CUT-WAY FEELINS
James Berry

Yu know him gone.
Children we know him gone.
Him gone lef de sun
fi walk tru yard
5   widdout him back-a-it.

Yu know him gone.
We know him gone.
Him gone lef stars like spears
from roof holes in we eyes.

10   Naked big shoulda not here—
dohn come an eat we food,
dohn come an mek mi curse
a-beg a lovin look,

Yu know him gone.
15   Children we know him gone.
Clay bowl dohn av
shavin suds pon Sunday now.
Logs dem alone hol up a house.

ALBERT
A L Hendriks

Albert dead Tuesday gone.
They say liver kill him. Liver should live!
Perhaps they say liquor and I hear wrong
for I never see any man take up waters
5   like Albert.

Today is burial.
Well sir The Society give of the best,
Miss Vi see to that, never mind she harass him
every God-day, everything correct,
10   and Albert shave, and dress so-till;
same Albert who scorn soap, and wear pant
till they have more patch than pant foot;
and the hearse big as Governor car
full up of flowers like Hope Garden—
15   for Albert who never own even a cycle in life,
walk everywhere, and bleed forty-chain to reach hospital,
Albert who never know buttercup from ram-goat rose.

EARTH IS BROWN
Shana Yardan

Earth is brown and rice is green,
And air is cold on the face of the soul

Oh grandfather, my grandfather,
your dhoti is become a shroud
5   your straight hair a curse
in this land where
rice no longer fills the belly
or the empty placelessness
of your soul.

10   For you cannot remember India.
The passage of time
has too long been trampled over
to bear your wistful recollections,
and you only know the name
15   of the ship they brought you on
because your daadi told it to you.

Your sons with their city faces
don't know it at all
Don't want to know it.
20   Nor to understand that
you cannot cease
this communion with the smell
of cow-dung at fore-day morning,
or the rustling wail
25   of yellow-green rice
or the security of
mud between your toes
or the sensual pouring
of paddy through your fingers.

30   Oh grandfather, my grandfather,
your dhoti is become a shroud.
Rice beds no longer call your sons.
They are clerks in the city of streets
Where life is a weekly paypacket
35   purchasing identity in Tiger Bay,
seeking a tomorrow in today's unrealit

You are too old now to doubt
that Hannuman hears you.
Yet outside your logie
40   the fluttering cane
flaps like a plaintive tabla
in the wind.
And when the spaces inside you
can no longer be filled
45   by the rank beds of rice,
and the lowing morning
cannot stir you to rise
from your ghoola,
The music in your heart
50   will sound a rustling sound,
and the bamboos to Hannuman
will be a sitar in the wind.

ON AN EVENING TURNED TO RAIN
Ian McDonald

Visiting the seaman's ward a hot afternoon
I discovered the old man dying, dying fast,
The rattle in him, the black crow flying near.
The walls dewed grey, the hard beds crowded close
5   The smell of deaths, the old routines of cure,
Of alcohol, rough sheets cleaned a thosand times, urine splashed
                              like holy water.
No one saw the dying of the old man—
All, all encased in dreams of life—
Until a nurse came with some tenderness
10   (I well remember her, she hard and tall as a post)
And took his hand, with some tenderness I say,
Hand frail as ash waiting for wind to blow,
And she held his hand until the black crow settled firm.
I wandered near, death's mystery a lure,
15   And heard the low words almost break his teeth:
"I live a good life, and now I dead!"
To write it straight as bone is not to say it well.
Slimed by black belly juices the tongue fell out of him;
That nurse stood and settled him and cleaned his vomit up.
20   I knew him well, a strong man in his day.
The black crow cawed, rattling a joyful wing
And so the old man died, leaving his words to me.

There is a bureaucracy for moving people on: they buried him quick
That evening, turned to rain.
25   Your funeral cart, my reader, will be more glorious than his:
Think now of your heaped flowers, not for him!
No man shall go naked to his cavern-rest,
A grey robe sheeted him, rough as cattle tongue.
A lead medallion twined his neck for long identity.
30   (So, old counterfeit Pharoah! They left you that last treasure!)
When the world overturns, they say, God will know his bones.
He had a pauper's grave, black hole glistening in the earth.
There the long trenches furrow straight between the graves,
Narrow moats with lilies red and sweet as flesh;
35   And palms wave above in melancholy green.
In rainy times the trenches swamp the burial places of the poor;
The rich man's bones keep dry on higher ground.
He had his retinue like any other man:
The grave diggers, brawny—young and laughing,

40 And the lantern-carrier, uncle of a thousand deaths.
    And myself, watchman at a distance, not near enough for love
        or work.
    An old moon coming up, a cold wind blowing,
    The rain drifting in, bringing the smell of the sea.
45 No one claimed him, no sons came.

    His words pursued me as I followed him.
    "I live a good life, and now I dead!"
    I puzzle at the old man's meanings.
    He was so certain when he spoke,
50 He had an idea in his mind I'm sure,
    He had to say his chosen words out clear,
    They almost broke his teeth to say.
    Silence was not good enough for him;
    The breath inside him screeched like sharpened bone.

55 Was it defiance that he spoke?
    Proud of living well in full enjoyment,
    Women feted, fondled, wine drunk down.
    Every pleasure tasted in his young and middling life,
    And now he thought of that and spat a curse at death,
60 Could that be it? Or was it black agony of loss?
    Of loss and bitter disillusion, his words an agony:
    "I live a good life, and now I dead!"
    So much of sacrifice offered up, no justice in return.

    Was that the thought that struggled to be said:
65 Each man who dies, he dies in desperation
    Like a stray cat strangling in a ditch?
    Or was it fierce eternal faith,
    An echo of the saint's calm prayer:
    "Let nothing disturb thee
70 Let nothing affright thee
    All passeth away
    God alone will stay."

    The ashes of the old man's words I taste
    I think of Gandhi in his hungering quest,
75 Of Hitler in his iron hate,
    Of emperors polishing bright swords of war,
    Of poets practising their songs of love.
    Beggarman, I think of you!
    The dark evening turns to heavier rain
80 My thoughts' confusion troubles me
    All, all are pity's children
    All will go out like flame.
    The water cleans the old man in his grave forever.

TERMINAL
Mervyn Morris

She's withering
before our eyes

and no one
noticeably

5   cries
We do

the hopeful
ritual

each day

10   we bring

fresh fruit
we prattle

and we pray
for hours

15   Her room
is heavy

with the scent
of flowers

THEOPHILUS JONES WALKS NAKED
DOWN KING STREET
Heather Royes

On Monday, October 18th,
Theophilus Jones took off
his asphalt-black, rag-tag pants
and walked naked down King Street.
5   It was a holiday—
and only a few people saw
his triumphant march,
his muscular, bearded-brown body,
his genitals flapping in front.
10   Theophilus Jones had wanted
to do this for a long time.

At Tower and King three carwash boys,
shouting "Madman!", followed him to Harbour Street
but, seeing his indifference, turned
15   and dribbled back up the road.
Down on the Ferry Pier a handful of people,
waiting for the boat, stared out to sea
but did not see
Theophilus enter the water.

20 He walked out as far as possible,
then began to swim, strongly and calmly,
into the middle of the harbour.
Eventually, way out in the deep,
he stopped,
25 floated for a while, enjoying the sun,
watched a plane take off from the green-rimmed palisades,
and then, letting himself go,
allowed the water
to swallow him up.

30 Theophilus Jones went down
slowly,
slowly his bent legs, slowly
his arms above his head,
slowly his locksed hair,
35 slowly.
Until nothing could be seen of him.
Some orange peel, an old tin-can
and a sea-saturated cigarette box
floated over his demise,
40 while nearby,
a kingfisher—scavenging for sprats
on a low current—veered down
and landed,
in a spray of sunlit water.

simple tings
Jean Binta Breeze

(for Miss Adlyn and Aunt Vida)

de simple tings of life, mi dear
de simple tings of life

she rocked the rhythms in her chair
brushed a hand across her hair
5 miles of travel in her stare

de simple tings of life

ah hoe mi corn
an de backache gone
plant mi peas
10 arthritis ease

de simple tings of life

leaning back
she wiped an eye
read the rain signs
15 in the sky
evening's ashes
in a fireside

de simple tings of life

THE SADDHU OF COUVA
Derek Walcott

For Kenneth Ramchand

When sunset, a brass gong,
vibrate through Couva,
is then I see my soul, swiftly unsheathed,
like a white cattle bird growing more small
5   over the ocean of the evening canes,
and I set quiet, waiting for it to return
like a hog-cattle blistered with mud,
because, for my spirit, India is too far.
And to that gong
10   sometimes bald clouds in saffron robes assemble
sacred to the evening,
sacred even to Ramlochan,
singing Indian hits from his jute hammock
while evening strokes the flanks
15   and silver horns of his maroon taxi,
as the mosquitoes whine their evening mantras,
my friend Anopheles, on the sitar,
and the fireflies making every dusk Divali.

I knot my head with a cloud,
20   my white mustache bristle like horns,
my hands are brittle as the pages of Ramayana.
Once the sacred monkeys multiplied like branches
in the ancient temples; I did not miss them,
because these fields sang of Bengal,
25   behind Ramlochan Repairs there was Uttar Pradesh;
but times roars in my ears like a river,
old age is a conflagration
as fierce as the cane fires of crop time.
I will pass through these people like a cloud,
30   they will see a white bird beating the evening sea
of the canes behind Couva,
and who will point it as my soul unsheathed?
Neither the bridegroom in beads,
nor the bride in her veils,
35   their sacred language on the cinema hoardings.

I talked too damn much on the Couva Village Council.
I talked too softly, I was always drowned
by the loudspeakers in front of the stores
or the loudspeakers with the greatest pictures.
40 I am best suited to stalk like a white cattle bird
on legs like sticks, with sticking to the Path
between the canes on a district road at dusk.
Playing the Elder. There are no more elders.
Is only old people.

45 My friends spit on the government.
I do not think is just the government.
Suppose all the gods too old,
Suppose they dead and they burning them,
supposing when some cane cutter
50 start chopping up snakes with a cutlass
he is severing the snake-armed god,
and suppose some hunter has caught
Hanuman in his mischief in a monkey cage.
Suppose all the gods were killed by electric light?

55 Sunset, a bonfire, roars in my ears;
embers of blown swallows dart and cry,
like women distracted,
around its cremation.
I ascend to my bed of sweet sandalwood.

MAMMIE
E A Markham

She would hold up her head though
fresh air still slapped her
about the face
as if she was an immigrant.
5   She should know better than to gate-
crash at her—now unnecessary—
age, a garden reserved to residents
with a future.
But a little bit of memory return
10   to sit with her
to share a *past* with her
and prepare a joke she could use
against her exile. The ships
which brought them here had seemed
15   proud and confident, mistresses
of the sea. Now they too
were scrap.
            A familiar wreck adrift
in the city where her husband
20   went missing, berthed for a moment
like a man from home. She was pleased
he was not the father of her sons.

HOT SUMMER SUNDAY
A L Hendriks

Especially on hot summer Sundays
my Grandpa liked to rest
supine in the narrow bathtub
soaking in curved cool water
5   sometimes flipping his toes
or, quite child-like,
toying with a pale green soapcake,
but mostly
staying motionless, eyes closed,
10   lips half-smiling,
limbs outstretched.

That hot summer Sunday
when I looked at him   -
straightly lying, lips parted,
15   silent in the shallow trough,
a foam of white, frothed and lacy,
set as new suds
about his shaven jawbones,
it seemed he might stir,
20   whistle a relaxed sigh,
unclose those eyelids,
ask me to scrub his back.

THE ORDERING OF ROOMS
Dennis Scott

I remember the mornings when she squeezed
fresh oranges into a golden glass
bruising oil from their skins
with her small, thick knuckles—
5   to this day my mouth is full of that
sweetness, its taste in the house
of a stranger calls up her love.

Mornings. As always, wakes at five.
I dream of him you know, she says.
10   (My father, who outran her into light
these three years now.)
Prays quietly in the empty room,
blows thru the house opening windows.
That too about her I remember:
15   a certain heat, the ease of her dancing,

my mother. I wish you every day
the kindness of the morning,
its certainty, its promise.
Prayers for those gone
20   before you to a joyful place.
The ordering of rooms
in strict and simple grace.

8
Gods, Ghosts & Spirits

OL' HIGUE
Wordsworth McAndrew

Ol' woman wid de wrinkled skin,
Leh de ol' higue wuk begin.
Put on you fiery disguise,
Ol' woman wid de weary eyes.
5   Shed you swizzly skin.

Ball o' fire, raise up high.
Raise up till you touch de sky.
Land 'pon top somebody roof.
Tr'ipse in through de keyhole—poof!
10   Open you ol' higue eye.

Find de baby where 'e lie.
Change back faster than de eye.
Find de baby, lif' de sheet,
Mek de puncture wid you teet',
15   Suck de baby dry.

Before 'e wake an' start to cry,
Change back fast, an' out you fly.
Find de goobie wid you skin.
Mek you semidodge, then—in!
20   Grin you ol' higue grin.

In you dutty-powder gown
Next day schoolchildren flock you round.
"Ol' higue, ol' higue!" dey hollerin' out.
Tek it easy, hold you mout'.
25   Doan leh dem find you out.

Dey gwine mark up wid a chalk
Everywhere wheh you got to walk—
You bridge, you door, you jalousie—
But cross de marks an' leh dem see.
30   Else dey might spread de talk.

Next night you gone out jus' de same,
Wrap up in you ball o' flame,
To find an' suck another child,
But tikkay! Rumour spreadin' wild.

35 An' people know you name.

Fly across dis window-sill.
Why dis baby lyin' so still?
Lif' de sheet like how you does do.
Oh God! Dis baby nightgown blue!
40 Run fo' de window-sill!

Woman you gwine run or not?
Doan mind de rice near to de cot.
De smell o' asafoetida
Like um tek effect 'pon you.
45 You wan' get kyetch or what?

But now is too late for advice,
'Cause you done start to count de rice
An' if you only drop one grain
You must begin it all again.
50 But you gwine count in vain.

Whuh ah tell you?

Day done light an' rice still mountin'
Till dey wake an' kyetch you countin'
An pick up de big fat cabbage broom
55 An' beat you all around de room.
  Is now you should start countin'.

Whaxen! Whaxen! Whaxen! Plai!
You gwine pay fo' you sins befo' you die.
Lash she all across she head.
60 You suck me baby till um dead?
  Whaxen! Whaxen! Plai!

You feel de manicole 'cross you hip?
Beat she till blood start to drip.
"Ow me God! You bruk me hip!
Done now, nuh? Allyou done!"

65 Is whuh you sayin' deh, you witch?
Done? Look, all you beat de bitch.
Whaxen! Whaxen! Pladai! Pilai!
Die, you witch you. Die!
Whaxen!
70 Whaxen!
   Plai!

SHABINE ENCOUNTERS THE MIDDLE PASSAGE
Derek Walcott

Man, I brisk in the galley first thing next dawn,
brewing li'l coffee; fog coil from the sea
like the kettle steaming when I put it down
slow, slow, 'cause I couldn't believe what I see:
5   where the horizon was one silver haze,
the fog swirl and swell into sails, so close
that I saw it was sails, my hair grip my skull,
it was horrors, but it was beautiful.
We float through a rustling forest of ships
10   with sails dry like paper, behind the glass
I saw men with rusty eyeholes like cannons,
and when ever their half-naked crews cross the sun,
right through their tissue, you traced their bones
like leaves against the sunlight; frigates, barkentines,
15   the backward-moving current swept them on,
and high on their decks I saw great admirals,
Rodney, Nelson, de Grasse, I heard the hoarse orders
they gave those Shabines, and that forest
of masts sail right through the *Flight*,
20   and all you could hear was the ghostly sound
of waves rustling like grass in a low wind
and the hissing weeds they trailed from the stern;
slowly they heaved past from east to west
like this round world was some cranked water wheel,
25   every ship pouring like a wooden bucket
dredged from the deep; my memory revolve
on all sailors before me, then the sun
heat the horizon's ring and they was mist.

Next we pass slave ships. Flags of all nations,
30   our fathers below deck too deep, I suppose,
to hear us shouting. So we stop shouting. Who knows
who his grandfather is, much less his name?
Tomorrow our landfall will be the Barbados.

LEGEND
Faustin Charles

Old Ebby, the *obeah-man*
Who lives on the hill;
The neighbours could not understand,
Why the clawing spirits haunt him still
5   After an exorcism by the priest.
It seems one night when the moon was full
Old Ebby initiated and entered a crab's skull
Then crawling down in darkness and rain
He traced the crab's steps circling his brain,
10   The amphibious instinct led him through a hole
Under-ground where he found a human skeleton
Clutching an ancestor-scroll;
From his twin-life, tangling, merging soul
He saw the separation and mystery of his birth
15   And the final fusion of his place on earth;
His racing mind could not contain
The multiplying creatures trying to explain
His lost life, forgotten for all its worth;
Then wildly scurrying through a cave
20   He squeezed under a stone gate leading to a grave
And there resting on a tomb
Heard God speaking from his mother's womb:
Like father, like son
Melting in the crab-nerve,
25   Fused into one.

COUVADE
Victor D Questel
(for Wilson Harris)

I'm a sleeper of a tired tribe
staring with a fish's eye
seeing the circle we draw
while pursued by quick eyes of night

5   here where there are always the caves
the need to avoid the net of stars,
the urge to capture the awakening
touch of feather or scale

threading through the embracing rainbow.
10   Now eyes hunt the dream of history
cross the bridge of tribes
trace on walls of memory
the war-paint's final riddle

coughed by a lizard—
15   Where is the Nothing of which the sages

spoke?

ROLLIN'-CALF
Louise Bennett

Me deh pon hase, me cyaan tap now
For Tahta John a dead—
De odder night one rollin-calf
Lick him eena him head.

5 It is a long story, me chile—
Me really cyaan tap now.
Yuh mussa hear seh Tahta laas
Him black an white bull cow?

Tree night an day him sarch fi it,
10 Couldn fine it noantall—
So tell night afore las him seh
Him hear one cow a bawl.

Him meck fi Figgins' open lan
—Doah him an dem no gree—
15 An see de bull dah lie dung
Underneat one guango tree.

Him teck a rope an tie de bull,
An den him bruck a stick
An him labour de po cow back, me
20 Tan a yard an hear de lick.

Him start fi lead i home, but when
Him tun roun fi go call
Him see de sinting two yeye-dem
A roll like tunder-ball.

25 Him go fi holler, but same time
Him feel a funny pain,
An when him look eena him han
De rope tun eena chain.

Massa, him fling i weh an run,
30 Him hear de sinting laugh—
It wasn fi-hum cow at all,
It was a rollin-calf!

Him jump Bra Caleb wire fence,
Him faint as him ketch home,
35 An since him come back to himself
Him dissa twis an foam.

Me cyaan tap—is a obeah man
Dem sen mi fi go fetch;
Me feel me yeye a jump—him mighta
40 Dead before me ketch.

KORABRA
Edward Kamau Brathwaite

So for my hacked
face, hollowed eyes,
undrumming heart,

make me a black
5 mask that dreams
silence,

reflects no light,
smiles no pretence,
hears not my brother's

10 language.
Let me without
my mother's

blood, my father's
holy *kra*, traverse
15 paths where yet

the new dead
cannot know that
time was evil,

but where dew's
20 ears prepare
for my coming.

Back
through Elmina,
white granite stone

25 stalking the sun-
light, the dun-
geon unbars. I hear

the whips of the slavers,
see the tears
30 of my daughters;

over glass
of their shattered
cries, feet

bleeding, I walk
35 through the talk
of the market,

flies clotting
round en-
trails and trinkets.

40 Low voices murmur
like smoke; the *kenkey*
pots, drinking

gourds broken;
Asafoakye dance,
45 clay smeared

over fear, round
their arm-
pits; the white

cock's neck sac-
50 rifice fouled,
life twisted in

anger. Now the
village is gone
the castle col-

55 lapses in cloud.
Here now are the
thickets; leo-

pards cough
dust, snakes haul
60 rusty coils

from the road;
broad Akuapim
calls.

Here Nyame's
65 tree bent,
falling before the

Nazarene's cross.
Bells silenced the
gong-gong;

80 then limped on
down to their dungeon.
Cocoa grows now;

70 my spattered
cloth flapped
in its sound.

Koforidua quiet;
goats doze in the road-
way: des-

My scattered
clan, young-
75 est kinsmen,

85 troying the years
with their chew-
ing impersonal stares.

fever's dirge
in their wounds,
rested here;

UNCLE TIME
Dennis Scott

Uncle Time is a ole, ole man. . . .
All year long 'im wash 'im foot in de sea,
long, lazy years on de wet san'
an' shake de coconut tree dem
5 quiet-like wid 'im sea-win' laughter,
scraping away de lan' . . .

Uncle Time is a spider-man, cunnin' an' cool,
him tell yu: watch de hill an' yu se mi.
Huhn! Fe yu yi no quick enough fe si
10 how 'im move like mongoose; man, yu tink 'im fool?

Me Uncle Time smile black as sorrow;
'im voice is sof' as bamboo leaf
but Lawd, me Uncle cruel.
When 'im play in de street
15 wid yu woman—watch 'im! By tomorrow
she dry as cane-fire, bitter as cassava;
an' when 'im teach yu son, long after
yu walk wid stranger, an' yu bread is grief.
Watch how 'im spin web roun' yu house, an' creep
20 inside; an' when 'im touch yu, weep. . . .

HELLO UNGOD
Anthony McNeill

Ungod my lungs blacken
the cities have fallen
the easy prescriptions
have drilled final holes in my cells
5 Ungod my head sieves in the wind
Ungod I am sterile
Ungod it appears
I am dying
Ungod I am scared
10 Ungod can you hear me
Ungod I am testing for levels
Ungod testing 1 2 3
Ungod are you evil
Ungod I can't hear you
15 Ungod I am trying
Ungod I can't reach you
Ungod my lungs blacken
the cities have fallen
head sieves in the wind

20 Ungod disconnecting.

FRACTURED CIRCLES
James Berry

my life once
a dancing leaf
took a blade through her stance

my life once
5 a seeking whale
spun it out in a bloody sea

my life once
a looking eagle
drifted in wing ensnared

10 my life once
a searching lion
flew when a shot turned her paws

my life once
a busy fox
15 rushed from the fangs of hounds

my life once
A hiding worm
leapt from flesh of fruit and jaws

my life once
20 a hippopotamus
gave the gun stop a pale red lake

my life once
A lamb
dealt a heart to cooking pots

25 my life once
a green man
wandered from white sheets

life I rage
in fractured circles
30 fill me a life

PARISH REGISTERS
John Gilmore

On the floor of the bell-chamber's cupboard
pasteboard, calf and paper
worms and roaches still defy.
Morocco labels, tooled in gold,
5   gleam like wedding rings in duppy dust.
heaps of paper, blotched and mottled
as the freckled features of an overseer,
list so many names:
Susan, here baptized,
10   "Child of Apprenticed Labourer",
her rôle in life predestined.
John and Martha, joined in wedlock,
Field-hands both, of Such-and-Such Estate.
Peter the fisherman,
15   died in the almshouse.
No other monument have these
whose labour built our land,
but yet the door is shut upon their muted voices
while in the church below
20   their posterity, serge-suited,
sit in mahogany pews
and worship an alien God.

MOONGAZA
Rooplal Monar

Two a'clack ah manin
moonlight shine
daag bark
Bow wow wow
5   fram de ole loco-line.

Look fram yuh kitchin winda
O Gad neighba! Moongaza!
lang like coc'nut tree
wid lang silva haan
10   red red red eye

O Gaad me fraid!
'E foot wide open
gazin at de moon in de canefiel'

Mule-bye run fuh he life.
15   Duck!
'Low Moongaza pass quick quick
fuh do e bizness
wid Massa in de berrin-grung

Memba granmudda dem peep
20   Moongaza in dem logie
when 'e do bizness wid Massa
an' dem fraid! fraid! fraid!
Neighba Stella picknie
dead blue in she belly
25   cause she see Moongaza
same night dem fowl cack crow
cook coo roo roo.

Memba watchman Djoko?
Drop. Stone dead.
30   'E mule tramp 'e,
kick 'e,
mash 'e,
cause 'e tek tree shade foh Moongaza.

Memba 'hole nigga yaad
35   sleep soon
when ole folk
see Moongaza in de canefiel'?

Me skin raise big!
Ow Moongaza! Moon . . . Ga . . . Za
40   me picknie! Me picknie

Cook coo roo roo
Moongaza done 'e bizness
Bow wow wow
'E leave de estate foh bad

45   O Gaad neighba, Lawd!
Moongaza mouth wid blood.

Ahwe picknie, ahwe picknie
Moongaza squeeze am out
yuh life
50   foh Massa in e grave!
Moongaza squeeze am out yuh life
foh Massa in e grave
Ahwe picknie . . . ahwe picknie.

SUN POEM XV
Wilson Harris

Blue is the journey I long to go
White is the gate I open to show
the sun my face.
Brown is the road that leads to space
5   where the sky falls down like the highest hill.

Dark is the river where green trees sail,
where nothing learns to stand quite still
on the visionary road across the hill.

Lofty is the spirit that waves on high
10   Like a flag of wind that is flown awry:
 it is visible now to my naked eye
 to my naked eye and my naked mind—
 the flag blows out and wind blows in—
 they are one and the same like flesh and skin.

15   My wood and my bone are burnt in the sun
I wave like smoke, crackle like gun
March to meet the starry ground
Where the camps are lit and the spirits sound
Their bugles for burning bone and tongue.

9
Her Story

SAD MOTHER BALLAD
Jane King

There's a woman outside singing
of the wrongs that she endures
how a man has made her captive,
fettered, childed, kept, indoors.

5 One day she cries I'm young, I'm lovely
I'm on fire like girls must be
but the man of my desire
quenched it in a freezing sea.

And my thoughts are like sea serpents
10 snaking up to sink below
sometimes I still feel the beauty
then I rage because I know

that another alien creature
soul-thing wandering through space

15 has invaded my torn body
to suck its life from my embrace.

These space monsters have me shackle
bounded by these walls, their home.
He brings bread, and I must feed it
20 but I want to give them stone.

Want to savage them, to tear them
want to cram their throats with stone
maddened with these buzzing voices
wanting just to be alone.

25 Now my singing voice is shattered,
now my throat is raw and hoarse,
mermaid songs it once had uttered,
now it curses, harsh and coarse.

CROWN POINT
Velma Pollard

The sea hums endlessly
Stars through the darkness
wake my hupentery peace . . .

". . . A see mi great granfather
5 jumping hopscotch and playing marble . . ."

I see MY grandmother praying

". . . Bless the Lord oh my soul
and all that is within me
bless his holy name . . ."

10 and the round green world of penny-royal smells the
room
through windows cool and sweet
And khus-khus from the cupboard counter-smells.

On the shelf her pan
15 a miniature suitcase black and red
with stamps and old receipts and dust
there too her bible large and black
its file of leaves in red
turned to us kneeling
20 this bible full . . .
God's words and other words
birth dates and marriages
and deaths

". . . and forget not all his benefits
25 who forgiveth all thy iniquities
who healeth all thy diseases
who satisfieth thy mouth with good things . . ."

Thus speaks my Gran
through this Tobago silence . . .
30 and recreates the order of her room
and recreates the aura of her God
and speaks so clearly in me . . .

Perhaps the clutter of my life
obscures her voice
35 Perhaps the clutter of my mind
frustrates her
streaming to my consciousness
Perhaps her mystic to me
waits my silence
40 waits my tomorrows' spaces.

OF COURSE WHEN THEY ASK FOR POEMS ABOUT THE "REALITIES" OF BLACK WOMEN
Grace Nichols

What they really want
at times
is a specimen
whose heart is in the dust

5 A mother-of-sufferer
trampled, oppressed
they want a little black blood
undressed
and validation
10 for the abused stereotype
already in their heads

Or else they want
a perfect song

I say I can write
15 no poem big enough
to hold the essence
    of a black woman
    or a white woman
    or a green woman

20 And there are black women
and black women
like a contrasting sky
of rainbow spectrum

Touch a black woman
25 you mistake for a rock
and feel her melting
down to fudge

Cradle a soft black woman
and burn fingers as you trace
30 revolution
beneath her woolly hair

And yes we cut bush
to clear paths
for our children

35 and yes,
we throw sprat
to catch whale
and yes,
if need be we'll trade
40 a piece-a-pussy
than see the pickney dem
in de grip-a-hungry-belly

Still, there ain't no
easy-belly category
45   for a black woman
    or a white woman
    or a green woman

And there are black women
strong and eloquent
50 and focused

And there are black women
who somehow always manage to end u
frail victim

And there are black women
55 considered so dangerous
in South Africa
they prison them away

Maybe this poem is to say,
that I like to see
60 we black women
full-of-we-selves walking

Crushing out
with each dancing step
the twisted self-negating
65 history
we've inherited
    Crushing out
    with each dancing step.

OARS
Mahadai Das

I am an Indian woman
with long hair,
a band of beads
across my forehead.

5   I paddle against desire's deep
slow-dark river,
sliding softly along
in love's canoe.

My words, slender oars,
10 bear my boat forward—
a keel of silk
upon the water.

My fists clenched
round these wooden
15 spears—I row
consistently.

Ahead—
the river grows
Churlish. Rapids
20 Threaten.

My bark of reeds
is frail, light stems—
insufficient.

The current is fierce.
25 A weariness seeps
Into my marrow.

When that time
comes, love,
will you rescue me?

I AM BECOMING MY MOTHER
Lorna Goodison

Yellow/brown woman
fingers smelling always of onions

My mother raises rare blooms
and waters them with tea
5 her birth waters sang like rivers
my mother is now me.

My mother had a linen dress
the colour of the sky
and stored lace and damask
10 tablecloths
to pull shame out of her eye.

I am becoming my mother
brown/yellow woman
fingers smelling always of onions.

THE LESSON
Merle Collins

You tink
was a easy lesson?
Was a
deep lesson
5 A well-taught
lesson
A
Carefully-learnt
lesson

I
10 could remember
Great Grand-Mammy
Brain tired
And wandering
Walkin' an' talkin'
15 Mind emptied and filled
Bright
Retaining
And skilfully twisted
By a sin
20 Unequalled by Eve's
Great Grand-Mammy
Living proof
Of de power
of de word
25 Talked knowingly
Of William de conqueror
Who was de fourth son
Of de Duke of Normandy
He married Matilda
30 His children were
Robert
Richard
Henry
William and
35 Adella

Grannie
Mind going back
Teachin' what she knew
Pick on de boss frien'
40 on de boss hero
William de conqueror
My frien'
Is your frien'
But your frien'
45 Not my frien'

Grannie
Din remember
No Carib Chief
No Asante king
50 For Grannie
Fedon never existed
Toussaint
Was a
Whispered curse
55 Her heroes
Were in Europe
Not
In the Caribbean
Not
60 In Africa
None
In Grenada

Her geography
Was
65 Of de Arctic Ocean
An' de Mediterranean
She spoke of
Novasembla
Francis-Joseph Land
70 And Spitbergin
In de Arctic Ocean
Of Ireland
And de
pharoah islands

75 belong to Denmark
Spoke
Parrot-like
Of
Corsica
80 Sardinia
Sicily
Malta
de Lomen islands
An' de islands
85 Of de Archipelago
In de
Mediterranean

Is not
No Nancy-Story
90 Nuh
Is a serious
joke
I use to
laugh at Grannie
95 Repeat after her
Till one day
Ah check de map
Fin' de spellin'
little different
100 To how
I did think
But de geography
Straight
Like a arrow
105 Tip focusing
On de
Arctic ocean

Den
Me blood
110 run cole
Me eyes
stay fix
on de Arctic Circle
Watchin'
115 Spitsbergen
And Franz Josef Land
Watchin'

Lower down
De Faer Oer Islands
120 In Denmark Strait
Unaccountably feeling
the cold grip of the Arctic
Noting how

by a cruel trick
125 Grannie's mind
Knew more of this
Than of a Grenada
Of a Caribbean
Which did not exist

130 A wandering star
Spun out of orbit
When the world
For an eternal moment
Went
135 A little too fast

Teach the slaves
And their children
And their children's
children
140 To know and live for
Our world
No new creation
Just a part
Of the great everlasting
145 Old
Arctic
And Mediterranean

And now
We
150 Consciously
Anti-colonial
Understanding all dat
And a little more
Will cherish
155 Grannie's memory
And beckon William across
To meet and revere
Our martyrs
Fedon

160 And Toussaint
And Marryshow
And Tubal Uriah Buzz
Butler
And the countries
165 And principles
They fought for
We
Will watch
William's astonished
            admiration
170 As he humbly meets
Fidel
As
In a spirit's daze
He greets the PRG
175 We will move
Even closer
To watch Morgan de Pirate
Hide his loot
As we start
180 On our budget

In this beginning
We
Will rewrite
De history books

185 Put William
On de back page
Make Morgan
A
footnote

190 Grannies to come
Will know
Of de Arctic Ocean
But will know more
Of the Caribbean Sea
195 Of the Atlantic Ocean

We
Will recall with pride
Our own
So
200 Goodbye William
Good
Riddance
Welcome
Fedon
205 Kay sala sé sa'w
Esta es
su casa
This is
your home!

WITHOUT APOLOGY
TO PROUST
Christine Craig

A sleeping girl
holds in a circle
around her

all the backyards, zincy fences
5 flattened to a smooth path
for Sheba and Nanny, riding
laughing through her cells.

In the sweet beat of her veins
Erzulie, Diana step smooth

10 on a carpet of mint spread from
her back-step pot, always tended.

A sleeping girl
holds
in a circle

15 daily dispersed grains of
possible made one smooth shell
for her quiet ear. Rolling of waves,
flowing of deep rivers in her time.

STILL MY TEACHER
(Miss S.S.)
Rajandaye Ramkissoon-Chen

I saw the opening flower
Still fastened with dewdrops
And I remember how she said
"In nature there is excellence:
5   Two reclining clouds
On a bed of sunset sparkle,
A drop of ocean,
Rainlines picking bubbles
On a path".
10   And she became my teacher,
Once more.

She had dusted her books
After the croptime,
When burnt sugarcane drops
15   Like wisps of feathers
To mark her shelves
With curlicues of ash.
And her heart, like with angina, ached
To make a gift.

20   "For you" she wrote. The cover jacket
Showed gaps like nibbled-out knowledge,
Daubs of fingers, tears
That looked like moth-tracks running.
The aged pages were the sanctum
25   To some poets' most inner thoughts.

"Shine! like him" she commanded
"With that heaven-light".
And I saw me
A coiled cotton wick of flame
30   Again, from her, drawing oil.

soun de abeng
fi nanny
Jean Binta Breeze

Nanny siddung pon a rack
a plan a new attack
puffin pon a red clay pipe

an de campfire
5 staat to sing

wile hog a spit grease
pon machete crease
sharp as fire release
an er yeye roam crass
10 ebery mountain pass
an er yeas well tune to de win'

an de cricket an de treefrog
crackle telegram
an she wet er battam lip fi decode

15 an de people gadda roun
tune een to er soun
wid a richness dat aboun
she wear dem crown
pon er natty platty atless head

20 an ebery smoke fram er pipe
is a signal fi de fight
an de people dem a sing
mek de cockpit ring
an de chant jus a rise, jus a rise
25 to de skies
wid de fervour of freedom
dat bus up chain
dat strap de ceaseless itching
of de sugar cane

30 We sey wi nah tun back
we a bus a new track
dutty tough
but is enuff
fi a bite
35 fi wi fight

an ebery shake of a leaf
mek dem quiver
mek dem shiver
fa dem lose dem night sight
40 an de daylight too bright
an we movin like de creatures of de wile
we movin in a single file
fa dis a fi we fightin style
an de message reach crass
45 ebery mountain pass

we sey wi nah tun back
we a bus a new track
dutty tuff
but is enuff
50 fi a bite
fi wi fight

life well haad
mongs de wattle an de daub
eben de dankey
55 a hiccup
in im stirrup
for de carrot laas it class
so nuh mek no one come faas
eena wi business

60 dis a fi we lan
a yah we mek wi stan
mongs de tuff dutty gritty
dis yah eart nah show no pity
les yuh
65 falla fashion
home een like pigeon
an wear dem number like de beas
but wen yuh see er savage pride
yuh haffi realise
70 dat

wi nah tun back
wi a bus a new track
dutty tuff
but is enuff
75 fi a bite
fi we fight
dutty tuff
but is enuff
is enuff

80 so mek wi soun de abeng
fi Nanny

WHEN HE WENT AWAY
Peggy Carr

I packed his cases full of
cotton shirts
and thick warm nights
while he carefully
5 arranged his promises
in the windows of our future

Reverently I touched that morning
when he left
his farewell trailing
10 from a plane
and blending with
the chaste white fingers of
cooksmoke
which stole upward
15 through the dew to
wipe the smudges from the sky

How cheerfully our love moved out
to live inside
a cold blue envelope
20 and like an orphaned street-wise
child
slept easily
between two thin indifferent
lines

25 Like sheathed claws
atop a taut silk sheet
his first lies probed
the boundaries
of my innocence
30 then
artfully his words
rehearsed to
a finer edge
until

35 "winter"
"riots"
"strikes"
and
"Government"
40 flicked smoothly from his pen
to quiver
in my hopes

Carelessly he tried to patch
my still-hot pain
45 with random ten pound notes
and pictures
of some grey defiant
stranger

My letters drifted into
50 slow soliloquy
and reassured themselves
like Job

A velvet tongue of
tired midnight breeze
55 licked the moisture from
my cheeks
then shook an old newsheet
awake
snuggled underneath
60 and belched the flavour of
too many lonely women
on its breath

Today I forgot to
tremble
65 to the rhythm
of the postman's
bell

THE LOADED DICE
Amryl Johnson

Throw de dice, girl, throw!
Dey say is pure chance wha' bring we here

Throw de dice, girl, throw!
When dey divided Africa, who getting where

5   Throw de dice, girl, throw!
Is now we legacy to pass from han' to han'

Throw de dice, girl, throw!
If we lucky life good, if not we in a jam

Throw de dice, girl, throw!
10   Is a risk all ah we hah to take

Throw de dice, girl, throw!
Is your turn to roll an' know yuh fate

Throw de dice, girl, throw!
We hope yuh number eh turn out too low

15   Throw de dice, girl, throw!
Like yuh fingers freeze, yuh cahn let go

Throw de dice, girl, throw!
It look like is 'fraid yuh 'fraid to know

Throw de dice, girl, throw!
20   Wha' yuh say, yuh eh believe in such chupidness?

Yuh say we hol' we fate in we own han'
Is we own fault dat we cahn get on
We bog dung by too much superstition
Blame de dice when tings dohn turn out like we plan
25   We hah to fin' de will to free weself
Leave de pas' behind, it dead an' gone but
let de memory give we de strength to push
fuh wha we want
An' if dey try to pin we back against de wall

30 take tuh de street so dey know we eh makin' joke
    Man to man we fightin' fuh we rights
    Is bottle, stick and brick fuh some ah we
    Gun an' tank fuh we sister an' we brudder
    in other countries

35 Is dah wh' yuh say?!!

    Throw de dice, girl, throw!
    Fling de ting out de dam' window

TO MY ARAWAK GRANDMOTHER
Olive Senior

I reach but a finger across the universe.
Distance is only space–time and we
exist in the continuum. Understanding
reaches to shake hands across history books
5   blood kinship may well be a fairy tale
    heredity myths mere lies, Yokahuna as real
    as the Virgin Mary, Coyaba as close as Heaven.

    My spirit ancestors are those
    I choose to worship and that
10 includes an I that existed
    long before me.

    I choose you
    for affirmations pulsing still
    in spite of blood shed or infused.
15 Baptismal certificates are mute
    while the whisper of a clay fragment
    moves me to attempt this connection

    I cry out
    to you.

10
Exile & Homecoming

NIGGER SWEAT
Edward Baugh

*"Please have your passport and all documents out
and ready for your interview. Kindly keep them dry."
(Notice in the waiting-room of the US Embassy,
Visa Section, Kingston, Jamaica, 1982.)*

No disrespect, mi boss,
just honest nigger sweat;
well almost, for is true
some of we trying to fool you
5 so we can lose weself
on the Big R ranch
to find a little life,
but, boss, is hard times
make it, and not because
10 black people born wutliss:
so, boss, excuse this nigger sweat.
And I know that you know it
as good as me,
this river running through history,
15 this historical fact, this sweat
that put the aroma
in your choice Virginia
that sweeten the cane
and make the cotton shine:
20 and sometimes I dream a nightmare dream
that the river rising, rising
and swelling the sea and I see
you choking and drowning
in a sea of black man sweat
25 and I wake up shaking
with shame and remorse
for my mother did teach me,
Child, don't study revenge.
Don't think we not grateful, boss
30 how you cool down the place for we comfort,
but the line shuffle forward
one step at a time
like Big Fraid hold we,
and the cool-cut, crew-cut Marine boy

35   wid him ice-blue eye and him walkie-talkie
     dissa walk through the place and pretend
     him no see we.
     But a bring me handkerchief,
     mi mother did bring me up right,
40   and, God willing, I keeping things cool
     till we meet face to face,
     and a promise you, boss,
     if I get through I gone,
     gone from this bruk-spirit, kiss-me-arse place.

THERE RUNS A DREAM
A J Seymour

There runs a dream of perished Dutch plantations
In these Guiana rivers to the sea.

Black waters, rustling through the vegetation
That towers and tangles banks, run silently
5   Over lost stellings where the craft once rode
Easy before trim dwellings in the sun
And fields of indigo would float out broad
To lose the eye right on the horizon.

These rivers know that strong and quiet men
10   Drove back a jungle, gave Guiana root
Against the shock of circumstance, and then
History moved down river, leaving free
The forest to creep back, foot by quiet foot
And overhang black waters to the sea.

"MIDSUMMER: VII"
Derek Walcott

Our houses are one step from the gutter. Plastic curtains
or cheap prints hide what is dark behind windows—
the pedalled sewing machine, the photos, the paper rose
on its doily. The porch rail is lined with red tins.
5 A man's passing height is the same size as their doors,
and the doors themselves usually no wider than coffins,
sometimes have carved in their fretwork little half-moons.
The hills have no echoes. Not the echo of ruins.
Empty lots nod with their palanquins of green.
10 Any crack in the sidewalk was made by the primal fault
of the first map of the world, its boundaries and powers.
By a pile of red sand, of seeding, abandoned gravel
near a burnt-out lot, a fresh jungle unfurls its green
elephants' ears of wild yams and dasheen.
15 One step over the low wall, if you should care to,
recaptures a childhood whose vines fasten your foot.
And this is the lot of all wanderers, this is their fate,
that the more they wander, the more the world grows wide.
So, however far you have travelled, your
20 steps make more holes and the mesh is multiplied—
or why should you suddenly think of Tomas Venclova,
and why should I care about whatever they did to Heberto
when exiles must make their own maps, when this asphalt
takes you far from the action, past hedges of unaligned flowers?

THE SEA
E A Markham

It used to be at the bottom of the hill
and brought white ships and news
of a far land and where half my life
was scheduled to be lived.

5   That was at least half a life ago
of managing without maps, plans, permanence
of a dozen or more addresses
of riding the trains like a vagrant.

Today, I have visitors. They come
10   long distances overland. They will be uneasy
and console me for loss of the sea.
I will discourage them.

AEROGRAMME
Philip Nanton

Each week
my father's aerogramme
bent double
blue with cold
5   bites into the dust of the morning mat

On the front three tiny fishes lie
stamped and flattened in their rectangular pool

The typewriter with intimate precision
has splattered the empty lines below

10   With lids firmly sealed
stiff as pressed linen
(no enclosure would survive)
lines for autopsy are clearly drawn

"To open slit here"

COOLIE ODYSSEY
David Dabydeen

(for Ma, d. 1985)

Now that peasantry is in vogue,
Poetry bubbles from peat bogs,
People strain for the old folk's fatal gobs
Coughed up in grates North or North East
5   'Tween bouts o' living dialect,
It should be time to hymn your own wreck,
Your house the source of ancient song:
Dry coconut shells cackling in the fireside
Smoking up our children's eyes and lungs,
10   Plantains spitting oil from a clay pot,
Thick sugary black tea gulped down.

The calves hustle to suck,
Bawling on their rope but are beaten back
Until the cow is milked.
15   Frantic children call to be fed.
Roopram the Idiot goes to graze his father's goats backdam
Dreaming that the twig he chews so viciously in his mouth
Is not a twig.

In a winter of England's scorn
20   We huddle together memories, hoard them from
The opulence of our masters.

You were always back home, forever
As canefield and whiplash, unchanging
As the tombstones in the old Dutch plot
25   Which the boys used for wickets playing ball.

Over here Harilall who regularly dodged his duties at the
    marketstall
To spin bowl for us in the style of Ramadhin

And afterwards took his beatings from you heroically
30   In the style of England losing
Is now known as the local Paki
Doing slow trade in his Balham cornershop.
Is it because his heart is not in business
But in the tumble of wickets long ago

35 To the roar of wayward boys?
    Or is it because he spends too much time
    Being chirpy with his customers, greeting
    The tight-wrapped pensioners stalking the snow
    With tropical smile, jolly small chat, credit?
40 They like Harilall, these muted claws of Empire,
    They feel privileged by his grinning service,
    They hear steelband in his voice
    And the freeness of the sea.
    The sun beams from his teeth.

45 Heaped up beside you Old Dabydeen
    Who on Albion Estate clean dawn
    Washed obsessively by the canal bank,
    Spread flowers on the snake-infested water,
    Fed the gods the food that Chandra cooked,
50 Bathed his tongue of the creole
    Babbled by low-caste infected coolies.
    His Hindi chants terrorized the watertoads
    Flopping to the protection of bush.
    He called upon Lord Krishna to preserve
55 The virginity of his daughters
    From the Negroes,
    Prayed that the white man would honour
    The end-of-season bonus to Poonai
    The canecutter, his strong, only son:
60 Chandra's womb being cursed by deities
    Like the blasted land
    Unconquerable jungle or weed
    That dragged the might of years from a man.
    Chandra like a deaf-mute moved about the house
65 To his command,

    A fearful bride barely come-of-age
    Year upon year swelling with female child.
    Guilt clenched her mouth
    Smothered the cry of bursting apart:
70 Wrapped hurriedly in a bundle of midwife's cloth
    The burden was removed to her mother's safekeeping.
    He stamped and cursed and beat until he turned old
    With the labour of chopping tree, minding cow, building fence
    And the expense of his daughter's dowries.

75   Dreaming of India
He drank rum
Till he dropped dead
And was buried to the singing of Scottish Presbyterian hymns
And a hell-fire sermon from a pop-eyed bawling catechist,
80   By Poonai, lately baptised, like half the village.

Ever so old,
Dabydeen's wife,
Hobbling her way to fowl-pen,
Cussing low, chewing her cud, and lapsed in dream,
85   Sprinkling rice from her shrivelled hand.
Ever so old and bountiful,
Past where Dabydeen lazed in his mudgrave,
Idle as usual in the sun,
Who would dip his hand in a bowl of dhall and rice—
90   Nasty man, squelching and swallowing like a low-caste sow—
The bitch dead now!

The first boat chugged to the muddy port
Of King George's Town. Coolies come to rest
In El Dorado,
95   Their faces and best saris black with soot.
The men smelt of saltwater mixed with rum.
The odyssey was plank between river and land,
Mere yards but months of plotting
In the packed bowel of a white man's boat
100   The years of promise, years of expanse.

At first the gleam of the green land and the white folk and the
     Negroes,
The earth streaked with colour like a toucan's beak,
Kiskidees flame across a fortunate sky,
105   Canefields ripening in the sun
Wait to be gathered in armfuls of gold.

I have come back late and missed the funeral.
You will understand the connections were difficult.
Three airplanes boarded and many changes
110   Of machines and landscapes like reincarnations
To bring me to this library of graves,
This small clearing of scrubland.
There are no headstones, epitaphs, dates.
The ancestors curl and dry to scrolls of parchment.

115 They lie like texts
Waiting to be written by the children
For whom they hacked and ploughed and saved
To send to faraway schools.
Is foolishness fill your head.
120 *Me dead.*
Dog-bone and dry-well
Got no story to tell.
Just how me born stupid is so me gone.
Still we persist before the grave.
125 Seeking fables.
We plunder for the maps of El Dorado
To make bountiful our minds in an England
Starved of gold.

Albion village sleeps, hacked
130 Out between bush and spiteful lip of river.
Folk that know bone
Fatten themselves on dreams
For the survival of days.
Mosquitoes sing at a nipple of blood.
135 A green-eyed moon watches
The rheumatic agony of houses crutched up on stilts
Pecked about by huge beaks of wind,
That bear the scars of ancient storms.
Crappeau clear their throats in hideous serenade,
140 Candleflies burst into suicidal flame.
In a green night with promise of rain
You die.

We mark your memory in songs
Fleshed in the emptiness of folk,
145 Poems that scrape bowl and bone
In English basements far from home,
Or confess the lust of beasts
In rare conceits
To congregations of the educated
150 Sipping wine, attentive between courses—
See the applause fluttering from their white hands
Like so many messy table napkins.

ground:
–Psalm 127
John Robert Lee

(for v.)

Now he is committing to the land.
He deposits in a bank all his labouring years
in exchange for what they'll lend
to own this simple plot of bush, rock-stone, colony of
5   worms.

Now he stands, roots-ready. No more tears
for a far country. He's come to terms.
He will clear ground into space for towers
and guard the loves that age has borne.

10   Let certainties of doubt make faith a firm
foundation. Fear will be sworn down
in the clearing. Peg squirming
boundaries of hate with iron hand!

Holy be this ground which he has torn
15   from the encroaching weed. Honed
cedars bind green edges of his gates. Up La Morne,
cloud pillars rise. Look out for showers.

Trodding drenched earth, foot in him land,
far bamboo-bird bugling, the man see clear
20   the raising of him tabernacle, Him standing
in the Sanctuary, peace passing on Him works.

STEREOTYPE
John Agard

I'm a fullblooded
West Indian stereotype
See me straw hat?
Watch it good

5 I'm a fullblooded
West Indian stereotype
You ask
if I got riddum
in me blood
10 You going ask!
Man just beat de drum
and don't forget
to pour de rum

I'm a fullblooded
15 West Indian stereotype
You say
I suppose you can show
us the limbo, can't you?
How you know!
20 How you know!
You sure
you don't want me
sing you a calypso too
How about that

25 I'm a fullblooded
West Indian stereotype
You call me
happy-go-lucky
Yes that's me

30 dressing fancy
and chasing women

if you think ah lie
bring yuh sister

I'm a fullblooded
35 West Indian stereotype
You wonder
where do you people
get such riddum
could it be the sunshine
40 My goodness
just listen to that steelband

Isn't here one thing
you forgot to ask
go on man ask ask
45 This native will answer
anything
How about cricket?
I suppose you're good at it?
Hear this man
50 good at it!
Put de willow
in me hand
and watch me stripe
de boundary

55 Yes I'm a fullblooded
West Indian stereotype

that's why I
graduated from Oxford
University
with a degree
in anthropology

RAMON REMEMBERS
Wayne Brown

Three pilgrims passed here one October night,
one of those nights of windfall and the moon
arriving late through separating cloud.
They came into the moonlight from the wood.

5   I remember the heavy shining of their robes
and their strange mules, the hump-backed, long-
     necked ones.
Men walking watch the earth, but these looked up
and on their parchment faces doubt and awe
10 played for possession.
                The moon kept up
its patient expurgation of the grass,
its bulge-eye roundly stared; but what they saw
if not the moon, some torn cloud and some stars
15 in my unsubtle heaven, heaven knows.
Dispassionate as ants they crossed the field.

And, yes, I should have called out; there are laws
of trespass, after all, a man had cause
enough to wring a reason from their calm:
20 destinations, occupations, home towns, names.
I did not call,
I stood and watched in silence, like a fool.

So where in the end they got to, what they sought,
I cannot tell, and would not think it worth
25 the while to go enquiring about.
Their business was the nightsky, mine, the earth.

Yet there've been darkening afternoons, since then,
that I've looked up from where the horse's hoof
arrows the bumping plough and seen them there,
30 stray-footed, hesitant, wearing that same air
of dubious obedience to a sign
eye could not fathom nor commonsense descry,

And ignorance of their ending sets me free
to think them unarriving, drifting still
35 (a thought which, for some reason, gladdens me)
over the storied mountains, through the world.

return
Dionne Brand

So the street is still there, still melting with sun
still the shining waves of heat at one o'clock
the eyelashes scorched, staring at the distance of the
park to the parade stand, still razor grass burnt and
5   cropped, everything made indistinguishable from dirt
by age and custom, white washed, and the people . . .
still I suppose the scorpion orchid by the road, that
fine red tongue of flamboyant and orange lips
muzzling the air, that green plum turning fat and
10   crimson, still the crazy bougainvillea fancying and
nettling itself purple, pink, red, white, still the trickle of
sweat and cold flush of heat raising the smell of
cotton and skin . . . still the dank rank of breadfruit milk,
their bash and rain on steps, still the bridge this side
15   the sea that side, the rotting ship barnacle eaten still
the butcher's blood staining the walls of the market,
the ascent of hills, stony and breathless, the dry
yellow patches of earth still threaten to swamp at the
next deluge . . . so the road, that stretch of sand and
20   pitch struggling up, glimpses sea, village, earth
bare-footed hot, women worried, still the faces,
masked in sweat and sweetness, still the eyes
watery, ancient, still the hard, distinct, brittle smell of
slavery.

WHEREVER I HANG
Grace Nichols

I leave me people, me land, me home
For reasons, I not too sure
I forsake de sun
And de humming-bird splendour
5   Had big rats in de floorboard
So I pick up me new-world-self
And come, to this place call England
At first I feeling like I in dream—
De misty greyness
10 I touching de walls to see if they real
They solid to de seam
And de people pouring from de underground system
Like beans
And when I look up to de sky
15 I see Lord Nelson high—too high to lie

And is so I sending home photos of myself
Among de pigeons and de snow
And is so I warding off de cold
And is so, little by little
20 I begin to change my calypso ways
Never visiting nobody
Before giving them clear warning
And waiting me turn in queue
Now, after all this time
25 I get accustom to de English life
But I still miss back-home side
To tell you de truth
I don't know really where I belaang

Yes, divided to de ocean
30 Divided to de bone

Wherever I hang me knickers—that's my home.

MAI VILLAGE
Edward Kamau Brathwaite

You see it rusting there
sauteurs maggotty six mens bay
small delightfully unspoiled
the guide books say

5   on a fair
day you can see the ancestors grey
headed guardians who toiled
like gully slaves to give their homes away

there was a fear
10   for a time that marcus malcolm martin & mahatma one of the sooth
say/ers from among the youth might have boiled
over boys will be boils they say

but they chew gum sitting on the wall in sunshine or in a sha. a. dow
steer clear of politricks letting the future pray
15   unto itself with garbage & kwashiorkor freakouts of tropical vio
lets sore foot shak shak & nigger blooming sirius

& jean rhys hummingbirds of coulibri decay

Notes and Questions

1: *Roots*

NAMES
Derek Walcott (p. 2)

Line 6: "Levantine"
These are people from the Levant—Lebanon, Syria, etc.

Line 14: "Benares"
This is a city in northern India on the River Ganges; a city sacred to Hindus.

Line 15: "Canton'
This is a major port of southern China, from where many Chinese emigrants set sail.

Line 22: "Benin"
A city in the south of what is now Nigeria; it was formerly the capital of a highly developed civilization, famous for its bronze sculpture.

Line 24: "the osprey"
This is a large bird, living near rivers and lakes, now rather rare.

Line 42: "the courts of Castille"
Castille is a city in northern Spain. It was formerly an independent kingdom, and then was seat of the kings of Spain who held court there when that country was launching its "voyages of discovery".

Line 43: "Versailles' colonnades"
Versailles is a town in northern France, near Paris. Louis XIV—the Sun King—had his famous palace at Versailles built in the seventeenth century. It is a symbol of affluence and European culture, but also of decadence.

Line 45: "Corinthian crests"
Ancient Corinth was a city state in what is now Greece, famous for its architecture and ornate stone carving. A Corinthian crest, carved at the head of a pillar, is a bell-shaped spread of leaves.

Line 54: "Valencia"
This is a city in eastern Spain, capital of a region famous for its orange groves. It is also the name given to a town in northern Venezuela.

Line 56: "Mayaro"
This is the name of a beach in Trinidad.

Lines 79/80: "Orion and Betelgeuse"
The former is a constellation of stars; the latter a star in that constellation.

QUESTIONS

1 This poem suggests a link between language and identity. Trace the different facets of that relationship through the poem.

2 How far do you agree with the poet's contention that this relationship is important? What do you make of the last seven lines of the poem, from "and children, look at these stars . . .' (line 77)?

3 Some names have "meanings"—in the way that, for example, Douglas means "dark water", other names recall places or events or famous people or even the day of the week on which a child was born, other names are "traditional", family names, religious names. Find out all you can about your name, why you were given it, etc. How do you feel about your name? What—if anything—would you rather be called? Write about your name—beginning with a straight factual report but moving on to thinking about using the material as the basis for a poem.

ROOTS
Michael Smith (p. 5)

Line 8: "Youtman"—youths, young men.

Line 29: "trenton"—Rastafarian term for pig/pork.

Line 43: "dashiki"—a traditional West Indian loose-fitting shirt, brightly-coloured, usually hand-dyed—deriving perhaps from African robes.

Line 45: "locks head"—wear dreadlocks, the Rastafarian hair "style".

Line 46: "smoke illy"—smoke marijuana.

Line 51: "dem itical"—punning rhyme, developing the Rastafarian use of "I" as the inner self, the ego.

Line 70: "Dem ax him whe im age"—they ask him what his age is.

Line 71: "Im sey roots"
He says roots.

Line 75/6: "Nuh roots/cause dat nuh belongs to I an I"
Not roots/because that (his given, Christian, Western, name) doesn't belong to his inner self, his people's culture.

QUESTIONS

1 It could be said that this poem makes the same point about language and identity that is made in *Names*, but through its own language and form rather than its content. Do you agree?

2 Why might "searchin fi im roots/a cause an explosion/between man and man" (lines 14–16)?

3 Might such a search not, in fact, have the opposite effect? Where does the poem suggest this alternative?

4 Prepare this poem for performance. In small groups decide—taking your cue from the way the text is laid out on the page—how it should best be read and performed. Be prepared to give a reading of the poem to the rest of the class, so that different styles and emphases can be discussed.

Ask your teacher to try and get hold of a recording of Mikey Smith performing this poem. Much of the power of the piece depends on that dramatic presentation and the way he stresses and modulates and enunciates he words *off* the page.

UNIVERSITY OF HUNGER
Martin Carter (p. 6)

This poem is one of a sequence that Martin Carter wrote in the early 1950s when he was deeply involved in the anti-colonial struggle in Guyana as a founder member of the original, multi-racial, Peoples Progressive Party.

Line 43: "is they who heard the shell blow and the iron clang"
Slaves on the plantations were roused each morning by either a conch shell being blown like a trumpet or by an iron bar being beaten.

QUESTIONS

1 Who are these graduates of the University of Hunger?

2 Their voices are heard elsewhere in this anthology; can you say where?

3 Identify places where the image of a march recurs.

4 How would you describe the overall "mood" of the poem: *despairing*, *angry*, *threatening*? All of these?

5 "They come treading in the hoofmarks of the mule/passing the ancient bridge. . . ." Use that wonderful image as the beginning of a story, it *doesn't* have to be related to the poem at all, just conjure up that picture and see where your imagination takes you. Who are "They", where is the ancient bridge? What lands lie on either side? Why are they "treading in the hoofmarks of the mule . . ."? Where are they heading? Why are they leaving? . . .

THE LAND OF LOOK BEHIND
Philip Sherlock (p. 8)

Line 23: "horologue"
This word literally means a timepiece, a clock, but here used to mean the routine of sounds associated with different events during a day.

Line 84: "Lubola spoke, a presence from the shades"
Lubola, as the next sentence makes clear, was leader of the original Maroons who established the Land of Look Behind. He is speaking from beyond the grave, from the shades or shadows of an afterlife existence.

Line 132: "Goombay drum"
This is a Maroon drum, looking something like a stool with a leather "seat", which is beaten with the hands.

Line 133: "Coromanti flute"
Coromanti was the name given to some of the peoples of West Africa from whom the slaves were drawn.

Line 144: "the Abeng"
This is a sort of flute or trumpet made from the horn of a cow, played by being blown through a square hole in its side. The Abeng or Abend was blown to warn the Maroons of impending danger or rouse them to attack.

Line 150: "red-coats"
These were British soldiers, whose massed red uniforms were intended to frighten off the enemy.

Line 163: "Volta"
This refers to the River Volta, one of the great rivers of West Africa.

Line 168/9: "Quassia", "greenhart", "bullet-wood"
These are all species of trees.

Line 172/3: "Funtumi" and "Kodia"
These were African warrior-ancestors whose spirits guide the Maroons in their struggle to remain independent.

Line 6: "trashes"—the remains of the sugar cane crop after it has been cut.

QUESTIONS

1 How many voices, excluding that of the narrator, speak in this poem?
List them and write a brief paragraph describing who they are.

2 Write another paragraph describing the character of Quamin.

3 After reading this poem look at Jean Binta Breeze's poem "soun de abeng fi nanny" (p. 132). What image of the maroons do you get from the two poems? How does that square with the stories your history books tell you? Why is the history of the Maroons in Jamaica such an important symbol for people across the Caribbean. Write either a "factual" response to those two questions or write a poem that begins from your thinking about the Maroons, Nanny and the "story" of "The Land of Look Behind".

QUESTIONS

1 What is the dominant mood of this poem? Find the words which help to create that mood. How do the repetitions of words and images through the poem contribute to the creation of that pervading mood?

2 What do you think is meant by the following lines or phrases in the poem?
a. "Their hands and limbs are but fragments/that walk and bathe"
b. "Who can tell when midday meets/their rest—they eat, they talk?"
c. Is this not the country of dreams/of tales told my ancestors/of a faith told by life.

3 What, do you imagine, are the characters in the poem "wishing, wishing . . ."? They are observed in this poem but we have no sense of them as individuals. Write a poem or short story in the voice of one of these workers.

TO MY MOTHER
Eric Roach (p. 13)

Line 22: "Golgotha"
This is the hill where Jesus was crucified.

Line 31: "decrepitude"
condition of being wasted, worn out, feeble with old age.

CREOLE GANG
Rooplal Monar (p. 12)

Line 2: "punts"—flat bottomed barges used to transport canes along canals in Guyana.

QUESTIONS

1 This poem might well have been included in the section of the anthology entitled "Old Folks, Death and Mourning". Why do you think it is placed here, under "Roots"?

2 Compare this poem with *For My Mother* by Lorna Goodison on page 56. There are important differences of tone and of emphasis between the two portraits. Can you identify them?

3 What does the poet mean by the final line of this poem?

4 This poem is a kind of biography, a telling of the life story of another person. The poet tells the story of his mother's life in such a way as to honour her. Sometimes biographies are written in ways that are much less flattering to their subject. Choose someone whose life story you know well or are willing to do some research on. It can be a public figure or a member of your family, or a "friend" at school. Write a brief biographical sketch of that person. See if that leads you into wanting to write a poem about them.

ANCESTORS
Edward Kamau Brathwaite
(p. 14)

Line 12: "homburg"
This is a soft felt hat with a curled brim and a crease across the crown.

Line 42: "Ever Ready"
This is a brand name of a company which manufactures lamps, batteries, bulbs, etc.

Line 43: "Vicks and Vapour Rub-like voice"
Vicks Vapour Rub is a vaporising ointment which "relieves the distress of cold". Here it is remembered as soothing.

QUESTIONS

1 Why, when the poet put on his dead grandfather's hat, did he "hear the night wind/man go battering through the canes, cocks waking up and thinking/it was dawn throughout the clinking country night' (lines 22–4).

2 Section 3 uses the rhythms of a Jamaican folksong *Sammy Dead*. If you were performing this poem, would you speak Section 3 or sing it? Why

3 Are there any songs that you remember from your childhood that particularly evoke that time or a person who used to sing them to you? Write about the song and the time it recalls. Choose whatever form—essay, story, poem that best suits what you want to say.

OGUN
Edward Kamau Brathwaite (p. 16)

Title: "Ogun"
This is the name of the Yoruba and Afro-Caribbean creator God, seen here in his role as divine craftsman.

Line 28: "gimlet"
This is a small hand tool used by carpenters and sculptors for boring holes.

QUESTIONS

1 The poet's uncle has a project that relates back to his ancestral past. Give an account of this project and what it meant to him.

2 Is it significant that he worked on this project on Sundays?

3 What significance does the project have for you?

4 Draw a picture of the mask or figure that you think Ogun carved (do your best, but no-one is going to criticise your drawing skills). Spend some time looking, hard, at the drawing you have made. Write about it.

RUINS OF A GREAT HOUSE
Derek Walcott (p. 18)

Line 1: "disjecta membra"—scattered remains.

Line 4: "gate cherubs"
These are small stone figures of chubby, angelic, winged children carved as ornaments to the pillars of a gateway to a Great House.

Line 11/12: "Farewell, green fields . . ."
This is a quotation from the English poet William Blake.

Line 13: "Marble as Greece"
Ancient Greece was famous for its marble statues and architecture.

Line 13: "Faulkner's South"
William Faulkner was a famous American novelist who wrote about the corrupt and decaying society of the southern states of America.

Line 21: "imperious rakes"
"Rake" was the word used to describe a disreputable young "gentleman" in the eighteenth and nineteenth centuries. Often they were sent out from Britain to the Caribbean in disgrace—hence their "imperial" connections.

Line 28: "Kipling"
Rudyard Kipling, a British author, of the late nineteenth and early twentieth centuries, was famous for his writing about India. He predicted, reluctantly, the inevitable demise of the British Empire.

Line 32: "men like Hawkins, Walter Raleigh, Drake"
These were all British sailors and explorers, all involved in the slave trade. Raleigh certainly also wrote poetry, and the other two were minor "men of letters".

Line 37: "charnel galleon"
This was literally a warship in which dead bodies were buried at sea.

Line 40: "the ashen prose of Donne"
John Donne (1572–1631) was an English poet and priest.

Line 44: "Albion"
This is the original Greek and Roman name for Britain.

Line 51: "as well as if a manor of thy friend's . . ."
This line is taken from the *Devotions* of John Donne. The passage begins:

No man is an island, entire of itself; every man is a part of the continent, a piece of the main. If a clod be washed away. Europe is the less, as well as if a manor of thy friend's or of thy own were . . .

QUESTIONS

1 "The conflict between outrage and compassion is the core of this famous poem, though its theme is Caribbean history." Discuss this judgement.

2 What is the significance of the quotation in line 51?

3 Derek Walcott is sometimes criticized because his poetry, at least his early poetry, relies so much on references to European literature and classical mythology. Other people feel that such a range of allusions and echoes enriches his work because the great literature of the past is part of the heritage of all mankind. What do you feel, in the light of *Ruins of a Great House*?

4 "No man is an island, entire of itself" . . . Begin from there, where does that idea—as well as the beautiful way it is expressed— lead you?

BACK TO AFRICA
Louise Bennett (p. 20)

Line 3: "Yuh haffi come from somewhe fus"
You have to come from somewhere first.

Line 5: "Me know seh dat yuh"
I know that.

Line 15: "Oonoo all bawn dung a Bung Grung"
Literally this means "You were all born down at Burnt Ground". Burnt Ground is a village in Jamaica, the line therefore carrying the meaning "You were all born *here*, on local soil . . ."

Line 25/6: "What a debil of a bump-an-bore,/Rig-jig an palam-pam"
What a devil of a confusion, rumpus, turn about.

QUESTIONS

1 Is there a conflict between the idea of "roots" in this poem and that expressed in Michael Smith's poem *Roots* (p. 5)?

2 Compare and contrast the language of the two poems.

3 The "common sense" position so forcefully and colourfully argued by the Miss Lou persona in this poem isn't shared by everyone, as we have seen. Miss Mattie doesn't get a word in in the poem; give her a voice, what might she say? Try and match the rhythmical pattern and form of Louise Bennett's poem—you'll find even that is harder to sustain than you might have thought—but don't expect to match her wit, skill and vigorous humour. The attempt is what is important, you will learn more by *trying* to write in that style than by any amount of reading *about* it.

origins
Kendel Hipolyte (p. 21)

Line 4: "strending"—this is an original coinage by the poet I think, conflating and echoing words like strain and stretch and bend and rend into a word which somehow suggests all of them.

Line 12: "Meteoroid"—literally a "fragment from the substance/of the sun" or other body from outer space, which becomes visible from earth only when it enters the planet's atmosphere.

Line 18: "aeons"—an immeasurably long period of time in terms of the development of the universe.

QUESTIONS

1 Find and explain what you understand by the following phrases or images:
   a. "the O of darkness"
   b. "long/before there was a time or Time"
   c. "a bonfire of speech"
   d. "flame into humanity"

2 To say that this is a poem about "birth" is only to begin to read it. How does the poet develop the images of birth and creation to suggest that something much "larger" is being grappled with here?

3 There are many "creation stories"—scientific, religious, mythological. How many do you know? Try and write one of them as a poem—thinking about what is involved in changing—compressing—a "story" into poetry.

ARAWAK PROLOGUE
Basil McFarlane (p. 22)

Line 28: "Coyaba of the wise"
Coyaba was the Arawak name for heaven.

QUESTIONS

1 Is the speaker of this poem describing a dream or a premonition?

2 Is that what he means when he says "It seemed I died" (line 26)?

3 Why is the poem called *Arawak Prologue*?

4 What do you know of the Amerindian people who lived in your country before the coming of the Europeans? Find out as much as you can and write a short essay, as if it were a feature in a newspaper or magazine, using any local or personal connections you may establish to give the piece added interest.

2: *Childhood and Adolescence*

FOR MY DAUGHTER YANSAN YASHODA
John Agard (p. 24)

QUESTIONS

1 Give an account of this poem using the terms "wonder", "innocence", "fear" and "celebration" appropriately.

2 What do you think of the imagery in stanza four? Part the stanza's charm is in the way its story is told, although the language is perhaps a little difficult? Why do you think the poet chose to write "knowing not which wind" rather than "not knowing which wind"? Consider the word "uncomb"— why is that so effective?

3 Talk about what metaphors are and how they work. Metaphors are a way of "showing" something rather than just "telling" it. Make up five metaphors for "ordinary" things or happenings. See if you can construct a poem around one of those metaphors.

CARIBBEAN JOURNAL
Cecil Gray (p. 24)

QUESTIONS

1 Where are the events described in the poem taking place?

2 The anger and pessimism in this poem are focused in the lines "his curse/at god's unholy sunday-school arrangement" (lines 13/14). Try to explain precisely what is meant by that phrase.

3 This is another poem in which the observed subject doesn't have a voice. How do you feel about the poet's attitude to his subject? Imagine yourself watching the poet watching the boy in the poem (!). Write a report of the process.

YOUTMAN
Linton Kwesi Johnson (p. 25)

Line 1: "youtman"—youths, young men.

Line 3: "site"—you see it?

Line 3: "ovastan"—pun on understand, to fully understand.

Line 4: "haffe faam"—have formed.

Line 6: "youtdauta"—young black women.

Line 7: "mite"—might, realm of power.

Line 14: "tares"—weeds.

Line 20: "scene"—(in this context) good.

QUESTIONS

1 Who is speaking in this poem?

2 What is his relationship to those he addresses?

3 How do you know? Does it have anything to do with the Biblical "cast" of his language?

4 The language of "youth culture" is fundamental to what this poem "means". The vocabulary identifies both the speaker and his audience—both share the vocabulary which would exclude those outside that culture. This is "rebel language" but you notice there are no swear words or obscenities. Each generation and each place generates its own "argot" or distinctive style of language. Draw up a list of words or phrases that "belong" to your place and age group. See if you can use them in writing a poem in which that language would be appropriate.

"BATTO"
Edward Kamau Brathwaite (p. 26)

Line 11: "hickey"
This is a copse or wood, the bush round about the village.

Line 16: "dodds"
Dodds, a notorious Borstal/remand centre.

Line 21: "cat-o-nine-tails"
This is a kind of whip with nine leather lashes that were sometimes encrusted with stones or spikes.

Line 29: "tro dung e cap an comman"—threw down his cap and commanded/challenged.

Line 52: "sen e to"—sent him to.

Lines 52/3: "out-/lorded"
This carries the implication of "outlawed".

QUESTIONS

1 Do you think Batto deserved to be sent to Dodds?

2 Is Batto something of a "hero" to the person narrating the poem? What makes you say so?

3 Every village, every school, has its own "Batto". Try and write a poem describing a Batto you know (she could be a girl!).

THE CHILD RAN INTO THE SEA
Martin Carter (p. 28)

QUESTIONS

1 Do you know any proverb that deals with the same paradox that this poem explores?

2 How would you explain, in a few sentences, the essence of that paradox?

3 "What every child wants is always/in the distance. . . ." Use that as the *final* line of a story.

A FAIRY TALE
Anson Gonzalez (p. 28)

QUESTIONS

1 Who is more of a hypocrite, "Sir" or the boy?

2 By referring to details in the poem, justify your choice.

3 Think about the two stories going on in this poem, what is openly said and the secret story of what is being thought by the boy. Can you think of other situations when such a "secret story" underlies what is apparently being said and done? Are those situations more common than we perhaps think? Is that situation in fact the norm? Try to write a sketch in which a similar spoken and unspoken dialogue is going on.

MEK DREAM TEK YU LIFE
Richard Ho Lung (p. 29)

Line 5: "pickney"—child.

Line 8: "mek dream tek yu life ya"—go to sleep, dream of better things.

Line 9: "Coo pickney nurse mumma swell wid child"—look how the child's mother, still nursing him, is already pregnant again.

Line 10: "an puppa cut stinkin' toe walk ten mile"—and his father walks ten miles to cut "Stinking Toe" (a strongly pungent kind of mushroom with herbal properties).

Line 11: "See Abel ketch wata ah give to Cain"
In the Bible, Cain and Abel were brothers, the sons of Adam. Cain became the first murderer when he killed Abel.

Line 12: "dutty tough"—literally, the ground is hard.

Line 19: "music a pound"—music is playing loudly, with a heavy beat.

QUESTIONS

1 Would you agree that, as in *A Fairy Tale* (page 28), the force of this poem lies in the discrepancy between fact and fantasy—the world as it is and the world as it might be?

2 How do you interpret the repeated line "scorpion kyah walk 'nancy web" (line 7, line 29)?

3 "scorpion kyah walk 'nancy web". Several poems in the collection make powerful use of proverb. Make a list of ten proverbs used in your district/family/school. Select the one that seems the most vivid to you. Begin to write a poem from there.

A LESSON FOR THIS SUNDAY
Derek Walcott (p. 30)

Line 4: "scansion"
This refers to the measure, the rhythmic movement of verse.

Line 13: "lepidopterists"
These are scientists who collect and study butterflies.

Line 16: "eviscerate"
This means to cut open or disembowel.

Lines 21/2: "She is herself a thing of summery light/Frail as a flower"
The implication of these lines is that there is a paradox between the seeming innocence of the little girl and her capacity for gratuitous cruelty to other living creatures. This illustrates the Biblical idea of "Original Sin" which runs through the poem, that we are all born "flawed"—as a consequence of The Fall of Adam and Eve—with the innate potentiality for evil. This reference echoes in the final four lines of the poem.

QUESTIONS

1 Try, as simply as possible, to say what the "lesson" of this poem is.

2 What do you understand by the image in the last line?

3 When Derek Walcott was a school boy in St. Lucia he set himself to follow a poetic apprenticeship; he would take poems by famous and accomplished poets and use them as a template, modelling his poem very closely on their originals. This, he argued, was the way to learn a craft. *A Lesson for This Sunday* might provide a good model for you to practice the rhythm and rhyme of a certain kind of poetry. Read the poem aloud to try and hear the rhythmic pattern—noticing how the poet breaks from it sometimes. Look carefully at the rhyme scheme, noticing how, sometimes, he chooses a half rhyme rather than a full "chime" rhyme, how sometimes he breaks the sense of a line for the sake of a good rhyme, so ". . . upsetting than a//. . . protestant hosanna." The theme of the poem you attempt to write may or may not relate directly to *A Lesson for This Sunday* but if you are stuck for a theme then you might choose a moral dilemma like that Walcott addresses. This is a difficult task, but worth the attempting.

TRADITION
Anthony Hinkson (p. 31)

Line 11: "in we day"—in our day/in our youth.

Line 21: "people t'inkin"—people are thinking.

Line 22: "deed in fait' dey is"—indeed, in faith, they are.

QUESTIONS

1 Why does this poem end so abruptly?

2 How does this poem relate in theme to *A Fairy Tale* (page 28)?

3 The poem gives us no description of the speaker but his speech—both what he says and the cast of the language he uses to say it—gives us a very clear picture of him. Bearing that in mind try and write a monologue that allows the reader a clear picture of the character whose speech you are "borrowing".

COLONIAL GIRLS SCHOOL
Olive Senior (p. 32)

Line 8: "madrigal"—a kind of singing in parts associated with the European middle ages.

Line 9: "airs"—an "old fashioned" term for a song or melody.

Line 10: "declensions"—a grammatical exercise, particularly when learning Latin.

Line 17: "debased"—made less pure, less valuable.

Line 22: "Steppes"—barren plains.

Line 26: "Marcus Garvey"—black Jamaican political leader and cultural visionary in the 1930s and 40s, he is a national hero in Jamaica now.

Line 27: "Thirty eight"—in 1938 political/labour disturbances in Jamaica and across the Caribbean were important events in the nationalist anti-colonial struggles in the region.

Line 28: "desegregation"—well into the 1960s in some parts of America black people were "segregated" from white people, kept apart in terms of where they lived, what they could do, etc. Desegregation was the process of breaking down those barriers.

Line 29: "Little Rock, Arkansas"— an important site in the Civil Rights struggle in America in the 1960s.

Line 30/31: "Lumumba and the Congo"
Patrice Lumumba was an African political leader who led the confrontation with Belgian colonial authorities in the countries that are now The Congo and Zaire.

Line 32: "Vachel Lindsey"—an influential American poet in the first part of this century whose poundingly rhythmical narrative poem "The Congo" reinforced and entrenched negative stereotypes about Africa and people of African descent.

QUESTIONS

1 The first line of the poem is crucial in understanding what follows; identify the borrowed "images" the poem's narrator remembers. Why are they felt to be so destructive?

2 What do you understand by the lines
One day we'll talk about
How the mirror broke
Who kissed us awake
Who let Anansi from his bag"?

3 The perspective of this poem is that of a woman looking back on her secondary schooling. Can you look back on your primary school days and write a poem or story drawn out of those memories?

MIXED
Pauline Melville (p. 33)

Line 5: "sallow"—pale, with a suggestion of sickliness.

QUESTIONS

1 From the evidence of the poem, how would you describe both the appearance and the character of (a) the mother, and (b) the father of the child in this poem?

2 What is the effect of the single word "Sometimes" at the beginning of the poem? In what ways would the poem be different if it wasn't there?

3 The poem tells a story—and suggests a whole set of cultural values—in a very few words. It works partly by considering what was left "unsaid". Can you think of other situations where "messages" are conveyed without words being spoken? Try and write a story or a dramatic scene about such a situation.

EARLY INNOCENCE
James Berry (p. 34)

QUESTIONS

1 How do you interpret the last two stanzas of *Early Innocence*? Is the poet excusing the cruelties of youth? Do they need to be excused?

2 Compare and contrast the treatment of similar themes in *Early Innocence* and *A Lesson for This Sunday* (p. 30).

3 Do you remember indulging in the kind of childish, "innocent" cruelties mentioned in the poem? Write about them.

3: *Folks*

GUARD-RING
Dennis Scott (p. 36)

Line 18: "barracuta"—barracuda.

Line 29: "smalls"
This is a small gift; very often a gift to a beggar is described in this way.

QUESTIONS

1 Is the speaker religious or superstitious or both?

2 Is it possible to be both?

3 One critic has written of this poem that it "understands the vulnerability" of people like the speaker. What did he mean do you think?

4 What is the speaker vulnerable to?

5 Legends of "rings of power" occur in many cultures. And rings are important symbols of allegiance and affection in our own times. Make a list of the rings you know about. Write a story in which a ring is an important element in the way the plot unfolds.

TRUTH AND CONSEQUENCE
Edward Baugh (p. 37)

Line 5: "Cinna the poet"
This refers to Shakespeare's *Julius Caesar*, Act 3 Scene 3 in which Cinna the Poet is murdered by a mob although he has explained he is not Cinna the conspirator.

QUESTIONS

1 Although this poem originates in an incident in ancient history, it is very much relevant to the contemporary Caribbean situation. Do you agree? How could that be so?

2 Do you think poetry has any connection with politics?

3 Do any of the poems in this anthology make "political" statements? Does this one?

4 Where do you draw the line between what is political and what is "private" or "literary"?

5 Are any of these questions relevant to an understanding of poetry?

6 This poem turns on a case of mistaken identity. Thinking about the issues raised in the questions above, use the idea of mistaken identity as the basis for a piece of writing of your own.

THOSE WOMEN
Grace Nicols (p. 37)

QUESTIONS

1 What impression of the fisherwomen do you get from the phrase "cut and contriving" in the first line of the poem?

2 The poem describes a memory of childhood. What qualities does it share with *Thinking Back on Yard Time* (page 83)?

3 This is a "memory of childhood" and a praise poem to the fisherwomen it describes. Think about the roles of women in your community, your family, your

school. Choose one woman or group of women as a subject of a praise poem of your own. It doesn't have to be long but notice how vivid the pictures Grace Nichols gives her readers are.

SHOP
Victor D Questel (p. 38)

Line 10: "sabots"—wooden shoes or clogs.

QUESTIONS

1 Why do you think Koo migrated to Canada?

2 Why did he keep his departure secret?

3 Whose suffering is represented in the last line of the poem?

4 "Shop" demonstrates how even the most everyday and mundane experiences—like going to the shop—can be turned into interesting poetry. Think about your regular routine—catching a bus, watching tv, doing whatever family chores are your responsibility. They provide you with the material for all sorts of writing. You might imagine an event occurring while you are engaged in those activities, something might go wrong and have unforeseen consequences, or just by "looking" at those commonplace activities and trying to write about them they may become "meaningful" in a way you hadn't realised. Try. If you can't start, start by writing an account of the activity you have chosen in as much detail as you can.

SAINT RAS
Anthony McNeill (p. 39)

Line 13: "the true island of Ras"—
The Rastafarian's vision of a
promised land.

Line 19: "inchoate"—basic,
rudimentary.

Line 22: "temporal"
This means earthly, of the mundane,
"ordinary" world.

QUESTIONS

1 How would you describe Saint
Ras's state of mind?

2 What, if anything, does Saint Ras
share with Theophilus Jones in
the poem of that name
(page 103)?

3 Does the poem imply that the
society should change to
accommodate Saint Ras?

4 Most communities contain
individuals who don't quite "fit";
outcasts, eccentrics, rebels.
Write, sympathetically, about
such a figure in your community.

ROUTINE
Malik (p. 40)

Line 1: "clock and move"
The clock is the machine at which
workers must register their arrival and
departure. The speaker in this poem
is urging those ahead of him in the
queue leaving the work place to hurry
and use the "clock" so that he can get
away.

QUESTIONS

1 What tone of voice should this
poem be read in?

2 Identify a phrase in the first
stanza of Anthony McNeill's
poem *Saint Ras* (p. 39) which
sums up the process which
Routine describes.

3 When the speaker complains in
stanza three that "is centuries
now/I in hey!" (lines 19/20), is he
just exaggerating in his frustration
to get away, or is there a sense in
which he is stating a fact? If the
latter, what other words in the
poem support your judgement?

4 "Routine" is a kind of worksong.
What other worksongs can you
find? Songs or poems about work
or trade often employ the
particular language of that
profession. Try and make a poem
or song, with the kinds of
repetition that worksongs and
"Routine" employ, about a kind
of work that you have some
connection with.

WEDNESDAY CHRONICLE
Pam Mordecai (p. 41)

Line 2: "almanac"
This is a diary or calendar with
information on astrological events and
seasonal activities, including the best
times for planting.

QUESTIONS

1 What is the relationship between the state of the weather and the state of mind of the speaker in this poem?

2 Can you see any similarity between the theme of *Wednesday Chronicle* and that of *Routine* (page 40)?

3 Using "Wednesday Chronicle" as a model, make a poem out of your own routine.

LIX
Edward Kamau Brathwaite (p. 42)

Title: "Lix"
This is a pun on licks, strokes with a cane, a teacher who gives his boys a good "licking".

Line 4/5: "madrigal"
A madrigal is an unaccompanied song for several voices.

Line 7: "v-8 ford"
This refers to the first mass production family motor car.

Lines 9/11: "mohammet/had come to my mother's black/mountain"
This is a variation of the common phrase "If the mountain won't come to Mohammed, then Mohammed must go to the mountain".
Mohammed was the founder of the Islamic faith, and tradition has it, while he was trying to convert some pagan Arabs, he was challenged to produce some miraculous sign of his power. He ordered the local mountain, Mt Safa, to come to him but when it did not move, he exclaimed "God is merciful. Had it (the mountain) obeyed my words, it would have fallen on us to our destruction. I will therefore go to the mountain and thank God that he has had mercy on a stiff-necked generation." The phrase is often used of someone who has been unable to get his own way and finally bows to an inevitable alternative.

Line 18: "let me not think on it"
This is probably a garbled version—as half remembered quotations often are—of 'look on't again I dare not", *Macbeth*, Act 2, Scene 2, Line 53.

Line 19: "god wot"—god knows.

Line 28: "the virgin of Guadeloupe"
Brathwaite writes that this is "a rare black sacred figurine of the Virgin Mary once taken on a traumatic tour of some of the Catholic communities of the Caribbean".

Line 44: "mahoe"—a hard, black wood.

Line 49: "no ting-link no shak-shak"
These are musical instruments surviving from slavery days when they, like the drum, were banned from the plantation for their African associations and their ability to unite the slaves in communal activities.

Line 58: "faulked"
This is probably a variation on the Elizabethan term "faugh", which was an expression of disgust.

Line 65: "martinlutherblazinpen"
Martin Luther was the German priest and church reformer who founded the protestant denominations, and was famous for his fiery writings.

QUESTION

1 Here's your chance! This satirical portrait of a teacher gives *you* licence to compose your own satire on the manners and delusions of a teacher *you* want to get back at! If you get into any trouble from this, refer the aggrieved teacher to me! On the other hand, it might be worth remembering that the best satire is worded in such a way that the "Victims" sometimes aren't quite sure if they are being praised or ridiculed. How do you think Charlie Chalkstick would feel about *his* poem? Do you think he would recognise himself . . .? Write on!

YUSMAN ALI, CHARCOAL SELLER
Ian McDonald (p. 44)

QUESTIONS

1 How do you interpret the final sentence of this poem? How does it relate to what has gone before?

2 Who or what does Yusman Ali hate?

3 Why does the poet suggest that Yusman Ali's capacity to sustain hatred is a "sweet thing" (line 26)?

4 Yusman Ali is in a way a cursed figure. Certainly he curses at the world and at his luck. Write a story or a poem that features a curse in some way.

PORKNOCKER
Mark McWatt (p. 45)

The title of the poem, "Porknocker", is a particularly Guyanese term for a gold prospector. The term is thought to derive from the barrels of salt pork the prospectors took with them on their journeys into the interior.

Line 9: "Longevity"—age, length of life.

Line 15: "pirouettes"—a twirling dance movement in classical ballet.

Line 22: "metamorphic"—a geological term for rocks that have been transformed by natural forces.

Line 25: "shard"—fragment or splinter or rock

Line 27: "basaltic"—from basalt, a black igneos rock.

Line 34: "millenium"—a period of a thousand years.

Line 41: "eldorado"—Eldorado was the legendary city or country of gold that the conquistadors searched for, often associated with the region that is now Guyana.

QUESTIONS

1 Try and explain what you understand by the following lines, phrases or images, in the context of the poem
a. Line 3—"a vein of the mountain"
b. Line 22—"the metamorphic rituals of stone"
c. Line 26—"the rock's memory"

2 The poem is to some extent about "obsession" and dream—identify and discuss those aspects of the poem.

3 The dream of Eldorado—of finding the city of gold—has fascinated writers for centuries. Write a story—or a poem if you like—called "The Dream of Eldorado"

VIRGO
Dawad Phillip (p. 46)

Line 12: "Eartha Commissong"—a well known Trinidadian social commentator.

Line 30: "aloes"—the bitter juice of a plant that is grown across the Caribbean, used in medicine and for cooking.

QUESTIONS

1 What is it about the way the story in this poem is told that makes it so distinctive? Some people would say it wasn't a "poem" at all—what do you think?

2 In the context of the poem, what do you understand from the following phrases,
Line 15: "yuh gyal excelled"
Line 23/4: "only that/Port of Spain wasn't New York"
Line 46: "I is somebody, Papa"

3 By the end of the poem Virgo has become a "character", a kind of eccentric. Several of the poems in this section of the anthology deal with such figures. Read them through again. Can you distinguish between the outcasts and rebels and the eccentrics? Try and think of a "character" in your community who might be described as an eccentric. Write about him or her.

SWEET MANGO
Andrew Salkey (p. 47)

QUESTIONS

1 This is a poem of exile. What similarities can you detect between the attitudes of the speaker in this poem and those of other "exiled" characters in this collection, in *Mammie* (p. 107) for example?

2 What does the narrator mean by "a land of fruit trees/to return to"? Is it just nostalgia for home?

3 When you go away from home the taste of fruits and other foods associated with home are especially evocative. What taste do you think you would miss the most? Why? What associations does that taste have for you? Write about it.

4: *One Love*

: FOR JOY
Dennis Scott (p. 50)

QUESTIONS

1 How can "houses spread out their sharp arms" (line 6)?

2 What is the "theme" of this poem?

3 How does the metaphor of the kite develop that theme?

4 The poem is an extended metaphor, read it again to see how it works. Can you develop a metaphor to describe your relationship with someone you are close to?

DIALOGUE BETWEEN TWO LARGE VILLAGE WOMEN
James Berry (p. 50)

QUESTIONS

1 Write an account of this poem using the terms "surprise", "outrage" and "amazement" appropriately.

2 The vocabulary used in this dialogue contributes a great deal to its overall vitality. What is the effect of words like "overtek", "downgrow", "forceripe" and "ramgoat"? What have they got in common?

3 Try and write a dialogue of your own between two characters in which a similar vocabulary can be employed.

MOMENTS
Robert Lee (p. 51)

QUESTIONS

1 How would you describe the *tone* of this poem?

2 What does the use of rhyme in the first three couplets contribute to the overall effect of the poem?

3 Why do you think this poem is included in the "One Love" section of the anthology?

4 "Nothing depresses so much as when . . ." Begin from there, with a poem or story of your own.

FOR A SON
Mervyn Morris (p. 51)

Line 12: "primordial"
This word means something ancient or basic, trailing back to man's earliest instincts.

QUESTIONS

1 How could the baby's "warm primordial gurgle" (line 12) have cemented the bond between father and son?

2 What does the father mean when he calls his son his "release from time" (lines 15–16).

3 Compare and contrast this poem with John Agard's *For My Daughter Yansan Yashoda* (p. 24).

4 This is a poem written by a father acknowledging his love for his son. Sometimes we find it difficult to express our feelings for our close relatives, or we fall back on sentimental cliches. Try and write honestly about your feelings for someone very close to you— father, mother, grandparent, brother, sister. Try to avoid using the familiar greetings card cliches.

BARRIAT
Wordsworth McAndrew (p. 52)

Title: "barriat"
The poem is a "description" of a Guyanese Hindu wedding. The barriat is the wedding party or entourage of family and friends who accompany the groom to the wedding.

Line 1: "Om shri ganesh, aya nama . . ."
These are the opening words of a prayer traditionally made at the start of an important celebration or public occasion. The simplest translation of the sense of the line is "Peace and Praise be to God . . ."

Line 19: "pandit"
This is a pundit or wise man learned in religion and Hindu tradition.

Line 23: "ghee"—a sort of melted butter.

Line 45: "the lahwa smoulders near the tillak"
In the weeks before the wedding, the menfolk of the bride-to-be's family go to the home of the bridegroom and bargain with his father and uncles and brothers over the amount of dowry that should be paid to the groom. This gathering is known as the *tillak*. In the week before the wedding, a "choir" of girls and women from the bride's family visit the bridegroom's home to sing ceremonial songs and make offerings of sacred flowers and burning scented woods. This offering is called the *lahwa*.

Line 47: "the kangan"
This is a ceremony which takes place before the wedding itself in which the elders of the two families or villages celebrate the coming event.

Line 48: "the maaroe"
This is the platform or stage on which the wedding ceremony takes place. It is often made of bamboo and covered with leaves or cloth. It is usually ornately decorated with flowers and streamers and cloth.

Line 48: "nechhu"
This is a ritual to do with the caste of the bride and the groom.

Line 48: "khichree"
This is the food—mixture of rice and peas cooked with coconut and spices—which is offered to the bridegroom at the end of the ceremony. He must eat a handful of khichree to signal that he is satisfied with the dowry that is being offered by the bride's family. Until he eats, they are expected to keep adding money and goods to the dowry. Sometimes the groom's failure to eat is taken as a sign of his greed by his new in-laws and arguments break out.

Line 49: "the badie"
This is a sort of altar, made of clay decorated in ornate designs with coloured rice, which separates the pundits of the two parties during the paw poojay.

Line 49: "and paaw poojay"
This is the argument or discussion of the pundits, one representing each family, as they sit on the maaroe. They discuss the portents of the marriage and argue niceties of interpretation of Hindu tradition and custom.

Line 60: "bhajan"
It is a Hindu "hymn" or song in praise of one of their gods.

QUESTIONS

1 Symbols are important in this poem. What is a symbol?

2 Which "symbols/never before understood" (lines 57/58) become meaningful for the newly-wed couple?

3 Compare this wedding ceremony with that described in the first part of *For My Mother* (page 56).

4 Either write a report on a wedding you have attended— write it as if it were a reporter working for the local newspaper—or write a story about a wedding.

DECORATED FOR A KISS
Ian McDonald (p. 54)

QUESTIONS

1 What do you understand by the terms sensuous and sensual? To what extent does either apply to this poem?

2 The poem posits two worlds, that of the narrator's men friends and that of the woman he courts. How are those two worlds represented in the poem?

3 The young man in this poem is torn between going with his friends and following his own inclinations. Do you recognise that dilemma . . . most of us I think will know the feeling. Use an instance from your own experience as the basis for a poem or a story.

WIND AND RIVER ROMANCE
John Agard (p. 54)

QUESTIONS

1 The poem's language and the way the "story" is told suggest human characters for "Wind" and "River" and "Sea"—describe them as you see them from your reading of the poem.

2 Try to explain *how* John Agard transfers human experience and characteristics to his observation of the natural world.

3 Can you think of a way you can tell a similar kind of story, using a human situation to describe or explain some "non-human" event or relationship—the sea pounding against rocks or the first rains after the dry season or the way one creature hunts another, for example.

WASTING TIME
Opal Palmer (p. 55)

Line 7: "Cho!"—a very useful all purpose expletive like (but not quite like) "blast", "Hell" or "Wow" that can be both aggressive and despairing.

Line 13: "galang"—go along.

Line 21/2: "dem yah man wan/oman call call dem"—all those men want/ women to chase after them.

QUESTIONS

1 Why does the woman speaking in this poem prevaricate so? Was she every *really* in any doubt that she would phone, do you feel?

2 How would you react if you were the man receiving her call? Why?

3 Take your answer to question 2 and re-write it as a passage of speech and internal monologue— that is recording his thoughts—as "Wasting Time" does for the woman.

FOR MY MOTHER (MAY I INHERIT HALF HER STRENGTH)
Lorna Goodison (p. 56)

Line 22: "petit bourgeoisie"—middle-classes.

Line 34: "chantilly"
This is a delicate kind of lace, named after a town in France where it was first made.

Line 36: "crepe de chine"
This is a wrinkled, gauze-like fabric.

Line 36: "godettes"
In needlework, a godet is a triangular piece of fabric added to a sleeve or skirt to "plump" it out. They were especially fashionable in the clothes of the 1930s.

QUESTIONS

1 What was your immediate response to this poem the first time you read it?

2 List the emotions the poem takes us through (such as joy, confusion, anger). Illustrate each one with a passage from the poem.

3 In the light of this poem, what, do you think, is the poet's feeling for (a) her mother, (b) her father?

5 Look at the passage of the poem between lines 52 and 65. By that list of "ordinary" activities the mother is made to seem miraculous. Make a similar list of the things your mother or grandmother does for you, her particular qualities or attitudes. Arrange them into a kind of poem.

FAMILY PICTURES
Mervyn Morris (p. 59)

QUESTIONS

1 The first stanza of this poem sums up the general feeling of the piece. Consider the word "prophecy". What does it imply?

2 Do you recognize from your own experience the paradox the poem describes? Have you ever felt trapped or stifled, even by people you love?

3 What does the speaker in the poem dream of escaping from?

4 Write a "Family Picture" poem of your own family experience.

NURSE GUYADEEN AND THE PREACHER
Ian McDonald (p. 60)

Line 25: "Mosaic law"—the Ten Commandments.

Line 37: "with, say, a month to go"—this poem is taken from a book length sequence called *Mercy Ward* all set in a hospital for the terminally ill in Guyana.

Line 57: "enema"—an injection of liquid or gas into the "back passage"—used to diagnose or treat certain illnesses.

QUESTIONS

1 Compare the ways the two major characters in the poem are described—one through metaphor and one through his language.

2 When we read of Nurse Guyadeen saying 'Good riddance" when she heard the old man had died, does that change our perception of her? What modifies that view again, at the end of the poem?

3 This poem revolves around the argument between two characters. When people argue they often employ colourful language and vivid imagery to describe—usually in unflattering terms—their antagonists. Write down a list of the kinds of vivid imagery used in arguments in your house . . . what does your mother call you when she's angry, what do you call your sister or brother when you fall out . . . Arrange those phrases to make a poem called "Family Naggings".

ONE WOMAN
Shake Keane (p. 62)

Line 11: "dutty-man"—dirty man.

Line 12: "seine-man"—fisherman, who uses a seine set.

Line 17: "hen-man"—hen-pecked man, or maybe poultry man.

Line 17: "fren-man"—friend man.

QUESTIONS

1 Consider the language of this poem, its particular tone. What does it suggest to you about the speaker? Can you visualise him just by the language he uses and his way of using it? Write a paragraph describing the kind of person you think he is.

2 Read Eric Roach's *To My Mother* (p. 13) and Lorna Goodison's *For My Mother* (p. 56) again. Can you detect any difference between a daughter's feeling for her mother—in the Goodison poem—and a son's as represented in the Roach and Keane poems? Can you offer any reasons for such differences?

3 Look at your answer to question one. Use that description and the "voice" in the poem to write a story in which that character features.

5: *Home—City Life*

LETTER TO ENGLAND
Fred d'Aguiar (p. 64)

Line 4: "jumbie"—spirit.

Line 18: "roti"
This is a soft flat bread which was introduced into the Caribbean from India.

QUESTIONS

1 How can "Money . . . mean next to nothing" (line 15)?

2 Explain the irony in the word "feast" in the final line of the poem.

3 Why should the sender of the letter ask his friend in England for "any news of what's going on here" (line 19)? How could someone in England know more about what is happening in the Caribbean than someone living there?

4 Imagine you have a cousin, more or less your own age, living in England now. Write a "Letter to England" of your own, describing your own life and ambitions and requests. You can either write it as a proper letter or as a poem in the way Fred d'Aguiar has.

Mi C-YaaN beLieVe iT
Michael Smith (p. 65)

Line 9: "siddung pan igh wall'—sit down upon a high wall.

Line 14: "me five bwoy pickney'—my five sons.

Line 16: "partisan pally-trix"—partisan politics.

Line 41: "dem lick we dung flat"—they knock us down flat.

Line 42: "teet start fly"—teeth start to fly.

Line 58: "bap si kaisico she pregnant again"
This refers to a rhythm pattern from a Jamaican children's game: *bap si kaisico pinda* (peanut) *shell*.

QUESTIONS

1 What, overall, can the speaker *not* believe?

2 What sort of character is he?

3 What similarities do you find between the speaker of this and the speaker in *Down Beat* (page 72)?

4 Mikey Smith has described how he gathered material for this poem, by listening to/overhearing people talking at bus stops, in shops, in meetings etc. Use that same technique to gather material for your own version of "Mi C-YaaN beLieVe iT".

NO MAN'S LAND
Gloria Escoffery (p. 67)

Line 2: "hummock"—a small hill.

Line 15: "pieta"
This is a religious painting or tableau of Mary, the mother of Jesus, holding the body of her son after the crucifixion.

Line 18: "Is there no way"
This is an echo of Jesus' statement "I am the Way, the Truth and the Light, no man cometh to the Father, but by me" (John, Chapter 14, Verse 6)— the implication being that such a tragic "pieta" as the poem describes could be avoided if the true values of Christianity could be applied.

QUESTIONS

1 Consider the vivid simile at the heart of the poem:
"whose stringy son, like a sucked mango seed/
Lies there no more use to anyone" (lines 12/13)
Why is it so effective a comparison?

2 What do you understand the poem to be saying in the final four lines? How do you answer the question that closes the poem?

3 The "story" of this poem has all the ingredients of a sensationalist newspaper report. Rewrite it as if it were that kind of report. What is gained and what is lost in that process?

QUESTIONS

1 How do you respond to this poem?

2 Would it make any difference to your response if *A Slum Dweller Declares* were laid out as a passage of reported speech, as in a newspaper, for example? Write it out as such and consider the differences. Have the differences between the two versions something to do with rhythms and the way we are "directed" to read the lines?

3 To what extent does the language in which the poem is written contribute to its effectiveness?

4 This poem voices a perspective not often so unambiguously heard in poetry. But nor is the other extreme experience often plainly represented. Imagine yourself fabulously wealthy, living in one of those luxurious mansions on the hill. Write a counter-poem called "A Mansion Dweller Declares". Try to avoid the obvious stereotypes.

A SLUM DWELLER DECLARES
Oku Onuora (p. 68)

Line 10: "moongs'—among.

Line 15: "food fi nyam"—food to eat.

Line 22: "hag pen"—hog pen/pig sty.

TRENCH TOWN SHOCK (A SOH DEM SEY)
Valerie Bloom (p. 68)

Line 1: "trouble deh ya"—bad news for you today.

QUESTIONS

1 Does the speaker of this monologue *believe* that "Knife-man always attack armed police" (line 31)? How can we tell?

2 Do you think it was really "di bwoy own fault" (line 9)? What makes you think as you do?

3 "A Soh Dem Say . . ." this is a poem about rumour. How things get distorted and exaggerated in the process of being passed from person to person. Have you ever spread rumours? Have you ever been the victim of an unjustified rumour? Write a story in which rumour plays a significant part in the unfolding of the plot.

4 Fear lurks in this poem like "the figure in the garden,/lost in weed . . ." What fearful image particularly haunts your imagination? Write about it . . . it might help!

AD. FOR A HOUSING SCHEME
Anthony McNeill (p. 70)

Lines 8/9: "z-/ros"
This is a pun on zero and row.

Line 20: "tenement"
A tenement is a large building divided into many small homes. The term carries an implication of referring to run down, overcrowded, slum dwellings.

RED HILLS
Wayne Brown (p. 69)

Title: "Red Hills"
This is the name of an affluent suburb of Kingston, Jamaica.

QUESTIONS

1 This seems at first a very different kind of city life from that endured by the subjects of *A Slum Dweller Declares*.
What problems do the slum dwellers and the residents of Red Hills have in common?

2 Explain the ironies in "roses bloom whitely here" (line 9) and "keep love in" (line 13).

3 Why can the residents of Red Hills "find no use for memory" (line 14)?

QUESTIONS

1 The poem's title is ironic. Explain the irony.

2 What might the characters in *Fewcha Gaan* (page 71) and *A Slum Dweller Declares* (page 68) make of this oppressive architecture?

3 "A poem of middle-class angst." Discuss.

4 The title of the poem is ironic. How might the builder/Real Estate Agents of the Housing Scheme have described the same properties in their publicity material?

FEWCHA GAAN
Fred Nunes (p. 71)

Title: "Fewcha Gaan"
This means Future Gone.

Line 4: "bang-belly nose naught"—
swollen stomach with nothing in it.

Line 9/10: "in a dim san' dash/bax"—
in a dark, sand blasted box.

**Lines 11/12: "bruk slate tight skirt/
tear pants"**—broken slates, tight (too
small) skirt/torn trousers.

**Line 13: "an' tick strap comin dung
de line"**—and a thick strap (to beat
us) coming towards us.

Line 21: "A fe me!"—This is me—
can this be my lot?

Line 27: "Babylon come"—The
police catch him.

Line 30: "eena cole stone cell"—in a
cold stone cell.

Line 34: "what a way dem teach"—
what an example the heartless state
sets.

**Line 40: "ship come   ship sink   'ope
gaan."**
The promised ship that will take the
Rastafarians "home" to Africa has
arrived—but that ship is recognised as
just a dream—hope gone.

QUESTIONS

1 The voices in this poem are
similar to other voices we have
encountered in this anthology.
Which are they?

2 In what sense does this poem
answer the question posed at the
end of *No Man's Land*
(page 67)?

3 In the light of your consideration
of *Truth and Consequences*
(page 37), do you consider this
to be a "political" poem?

4 Imagine you are a lawyer
defending the narrator of
"Fewcha Gaan" in a law court. It
is an appeal against his sentence.
You must try and convince the
judge that there are "mitigating
circumstances" which justify
leniency. Write the speech or
statement you would make.

DOWN BEAT
Victor D Questel (p. 72)

Line 9: "Ma Dolly fence"—Mother
Dolly's fence.

Line 11: "to buss"—to bust (break/
collapse).

Line 13: "to ask Chin for trus"—to
ask Chin (the ubiquitous Chinese
shopkeeper) for trust—that is, for
credit.

Line 21: "a fete"—a party.

Line 26: "meh sweet mas"—my
masquerade costume.

Line 31: "the latest rake"—the latest
racket for making money.

Line 36: "Talking ol'-talk"—
reminiscing, joking.

**Lines 61/2: "While the Redding
sitting on the dock."**
The reference here is to the great
American rhythm 'n blues singer Otis
Redding and his most famous song
Sitting on the Dock of the Bay.

Line 68: "The lime"—the promenade
of hustlers.

Line 81: "I calling dat George"—I'm accusing George (a barman) of . . .

QUESTIONS

1 What sort of life does the speaker of the poem lead?

2 How much do the rhythms of this poem contribute to an understanding of it?

3 This hustling, strutting street-wise Saga-boy is a fairly unattractive character (or seems so to a middle aged old fogey like me!) but he has his admirers and his female counterparts . . . try and write a voice-portrait of her.

LAVENTILLE
Derek Walcott (p. 74)

Title: "Laventille"
This is a shanty town slum on the hills overlooking Port-of-Spain, Trinidad.

Line 3: "Rio's favelas"
These are slums in Rio de Janeiro which was, until 1960, the capital city of Brazil.

Line 9: "Belmont, Woodbrook, Maraval, St Clair'
These are all middle-class suburbs of Port-of-Spain which occupy much lower ground than Laventille.

Line 60: "supercilious"
This means superior in manner, contemptuous.

Line 61: "rachitic"
This means affected by the disease called rickets. The word also suggests rachet—as in rachet knife—an echo picked up in the next line.

Line 83: "amnesiac"
This is something that causes a loss of memory.

Line 89: "cerements"
Cerements are burial clothes or sheets in which a corpse is wrapped.

QUESTIONS

1 Consider the references to the "middle passage" in this poem. What use is the poet making of the metaphor? Assess the importance of that metaphor to our understanding of the poem.

2 Notice the use the poet makes of rhyme in this poem. How does it affect the tone and tenor of the poem?

3 "We left/somewhere a life we never found,/customs and gods that are not born again. . . ." What do you understand by those wonderfully resonant lines? Use your answer to that question as the starting point for a story or poem of your own.

SONNET TO NEW FLOWERS
Mahadai Das (p. 76)

QUESTIONS

1 Where do you think this poem is set? Use details from the text to support your answer. Does it matter if we can't locate the setting precisely?

2 What, in the context of the poem, do you understand by the words or phrases?
(a) "Bricknude",
(b) ". . . Black flowers materialise late/from the dark, wounds in their sides."
(c) "hope, absent watercan . . ."

3 A well known contemporary British poet recently defined a 1990s sonnet as being just, "fourteen lines and rhymes". Using that very loose, open, definition, write a sonnet about your city/town/village.

SUNDAY CROSSES
Jean Goulbourne (p. 77)

QUESTIONS

1 The poet plays with the reader's sympathies in this poem by the way she describes both the Rastaman and the would-be customer. How does she do that? Is it a "fair" portrait she gives us of either character? Does it matter if it's "fair"?

2 Discuss the poem's title, "Sunday Crosses" and the way it's associations are developed through the poem.

3 Who opens the next door? What happens? Write about it.

6: *Home—Country Life*

THE DUST
Edward Kamau Brathwaite (p. 80)

Line 72: "Caroline Lee an' the Six Weeks"
These are varieties of vegetables.

Line 82: "yellowin' mustard gas"
In the First World War poisonous gas was used by both sides as a weapon against infantry. It "floated" in yellowish green clouds across the battlefields. Soldiers who were caught in such an attack but survived were often permanently scarred with a yellowish tinge to their skins and the whites of their eyes. Sometimes the gas caused men—like "Mr Gilkes" (line 81)—to become impotent.

Line 95: "the writin han' pun the wall"
This phrase is a version of the lines from the Old Testament (Daniel, Chapter 5) which describes the downfall of Belshazzar, a powerful king. As he drank from holy vessels stolen from the Temple in Jerusalem a hand miraculously appeared and wrote a message which foretold Belshazzar's imminent death. Daniel, the prophet, was the only man able to read this "writing on the wall". That phrase is commonly used now to mean that a person's fate is sealed, that they will get their just deserts.

Line 142/3: "Confederation"
This is an ironic reference to both the Confederation of Southern States (which broke away from the USA in the 1860s because they did not want to abolish slavery—their rebellion

was finally crushed in the American Civil War) and to the West Indian Federation (which broke up with much argument and recrimination among the region's politicians).

QUESTIONS

1 This poem consists entirely of dialogue. How many voices speak? List them.

2 Write a short paragraph describing each character, what they look like, how old they are, what they or their menfolk do for a living, etc. Do you know people like these?

3 The poem "considers some most serious and fundamental matters of religion, morality and philosophy, yet none of the characters can have had more than very basic schooling". Discuss.

4 Would you say that the awe and deep fear that Miss Olive's reaction to the mystery of the volcano reveals is related to the "vulnerability" that the speaker in *Guard-Ring* (page 36) betrays? Are they similar characters?

5 Select a line or an image or an idea from this poem to build a piece of your own writing upon. Read the poem carefully, at least three times, before you decide what your starting point will be. Then see where your imagination—or desperation—leads you.

THINKING BACK ON YARD TIME
James Berry (p. 83)

QUESTIONS

1 The poem is called *Thinking Back on Yard Time*. Why is it written in the present tense?

2 How old are "we" in this poem? How do you know?

3 Another poem of memory . . . "lost in togetherness". Who are your friends? How do you distinguish between real friends and others? What do you do together that sets you apart? Write about it.

WHEN MOON SHINE
Paul Keens-Douglas (p. 84)

Lines 2–5:
This is a riddle, a traditional way of greeting a friend.

Line 7: "teafin"—stealing.

Line 14: "Tanti"—auntie.

Line 23: "Boy, we must kill priest, we have cuss?"
Boy, we seem to have a spell of continual bad luck tonight, things aren't working in our favour.

Line 33: "he wutless for so"—he's worthless, in truth.

Line 47: "me belly near bus' with laugh"—my belly nearly burst with laughing.

QUESTIONS

1 *When Moon Shine* offers us a "slice of life". How does the language of the poem contribute to the "naturalness' of the scenes represented?

2 There is a riddle at the beginning of the poem. Explain why the answer to it is coconut.

3 Why is the poem entitled *When Moon Shine*?

4 Try to write a "Nanci story" of your own in the style of "When Moon Shine".

A SEA-CHANTEY
Derek Walcott (p. 86)

Title: "A Sea-Chantey"
A sea shanty is a work song sung by sailors.

**Epigraph: "La, tout n'est qu'ordre et beauté,
Luxe, calme, et volupte."**
This quotation is taken from *L'Invitation au Voyage* by Baudelaire, a nineteenth century French poet. The lines mean: "In that place, there is only order and beauty, tranquillity, calm and sensuousness".

Line 4: "Voyelles"—vowels (French).

Line 17: "Shaft of Odysseus"
On an epic voyage, Odysseus, a hero of Greek mythology, managed to resist the deadly songs of the sirens, mermaids who lured sailors to their deaths on rocks. He did this by tying himself to the mast of his ship. This mast is the "shaft" referred to in this line.

Line 18: "Cyclopic volcanoes"
The Cyclops was a mythical monster with one eye in the centre of its forehead.

Line 21: "Flight and Phyllis"
These are the names of ships.

Line 27: "Repos donnez a cils . . ."
This was taken from *Grand Testament* by François Villon, a fifteenth century French poet. The original line was part of a poetic epitaph and read "Repos eternal donne a cil", which can be translated as "Give eternal rest to the soul".

Line 39: "Barques"
A barque is a two masted sailing ships.

Line 44: "Leviathan"
This is the whale or giant sea monster and it is mentioned in *The Bible* (Psalm 104, v. 26).

Line 66: "portages"
A portage is a contract or customary right to carry cargo between two ports.

Line 68: "tartness"
This means a bitter, sour taste.

QUESTIONS

1 This poem is written as a kind of praise poem and as a kind of prayer. What is the poet celebrating?

2 Consider the following images. How do they contribute to the overall effect of the poem:
"Yachts tranquil as lilies" (line 7)
"Quiet, the fury of their ropes" (line 30)
"The scales fall from him
In a tinkle of church-bells" (lines 52/3)

"The music curls, dwindling
Like smoke from blue galleys"
(lines 60/1).

3 What do you understand by the
line "the amen of calm waters"
(line 78)? Why is it repeated three
times at the end of the poem?

4 Look at the lists in this poem—
the alliteration in the opening
lines and the vivid list of qualities
between lines 63 and 73. What
turns a list into a poem? Using
your answer to that question try
and write a "list poem" about
somewhere or something you
know very well.

THE TOURISTS
Wayne Brown (p. 87)

Line 14: "seine"—a fishing net.

QUESTIONS

1 There is a sudden change of tone
somewhere in this poem. Identify
it and comment on its effect.

2 Does the poet welcome the
tourists, do you feel?

3 As this poem suggests. Tourism is
a double edged sword as far as
most Caribbean societies are
concerned, in some ways a very
welcome means of earning money
but inevitably distorting the way
society develops. Either write a
poem of your own called "The
Tourists" or write an essay on
Tourism, looking at the
advantages and disadvantages of
the industry from your point of
view.

RICE
Martin Carter (p. 88)

Line 8: "padi"
This is rice, before it has been
threshed, grown in padi-fields.

QUESTIONS

1 What sort of personality is the
farmer described in this poem? Is
he optimistic or pessimistic,
straight-forward or cunning,
careful or reckless?

2 Consider the shape of this poem.
Why do the lines break where
they do?

3 Who wrote of seeing "a world in
a grain of sand . . ."? The world
in a grain of rice might be very
different . . . Think about it.
Write your own poem "Rice".

AIRY HALL ICONOGRAPHY
Fred d'Aguiar (p. 88)

The poem is from a sequence called
"Airy Hall", all drawing on the poet's
memory of and feelings about the
village in Guyana where he grew up.

Title: "Iconography"—pictures or
symbols distinctive of and particular
to a person or place.

Line 4: "ambrosia"—literally "the
food of the gods" but applied to
anything especially pleasant to eat.

Line 12: "Myrrh"—a scented resin
used in perfumes and medicine. One
of the gifts of the "three wise men" to
the infant Jesus in the nativity scene.

Line 17: "frankincense"—a very high quality, distinctively perfumed, incense. Another of the gifts of the Magi in the nativity story.

QUESTIONS

1 In some ways this is quite a "formal" poem—its a list of fruits and vegetables followed by a "description" of their qualities or effects. How does the form of the poem help the poet to achieve his effects?

2 The poem uses some very interesting imagery—engaging the reader's sense of taste and smell as well as sight—identify examples of those images and describe their effects.

3 Using this poem as a model, construct an "iconography" of your self or your school or your home or district or of another person. Select important images or pictures about them and develop or elaborate that picture in a second line of "description", as the poet of "Airy Hall Iconography" has.

"THE FISHERMEN" (FROM SUN POEM)
Edward Kamau Brathwaite (p. 89)

QUESTIONS

1 Trace the comparison of the fishermen with priests in this poem. How successful do you find the comparison?

2 Is this really a poem? Is it rather a prose-poem? How would you define a prose-poem?

3 Is the piece punctuated in an unusual way? What is the effect of the punctuation.

4 Fishermen have a particular status in Caribbean mythology; why should that be so? See if you can find other stories and poems that take fishermen as their central characters. Try and write a poem of your own called "The Fishermen".

PELTING BEES
Ian McDonald (p. 90)

Line 1: "samans"
This is a species of tree.

QUESTIONS

1 How does this poem relate to *Early Innocence* (page 34)?

2 The poet manages to make the scene so vivid to the reader. How does he do that? Look at his use of adjectives?

3 Try and write a second stanza following on from the events described in this poem, using your own experience as far as possible.

IN THE GENTLE AFTERNOON
Royston Ellis (p. 90)

QUESTIONS

1 Contrast the life described in this poem and *Thinking Back on Yard Time* with that in *A Slum Dweller Declares*.

2 How can we reconcile such contrasts? Do we need to?

3 Are such questions relevant to the study of poetry? Do they affect our reading of this poem? If so, in what ways?

4 "late in the afternoon on Friday. . . ." How would your account of that time differ from that represented in the poem? Write about it.

LETTER TO ENGLAND
Bruce St John (p. 91)

Line 15: "Brag pun"—Boast to.

Line 17: "t'ree"—three.

QUESTIONS

1 What kind of person is writing this "letter"? Write a paragraph about her. Is she like any other characters you have encountered in this anthology?

2 Compare and contrast this poem with *Letter to England* by Frederick d'Aguiar (p. 64).

3 Using what you know of England now, and the images you have of the way young people of West Indian background live there, imagine you are the cousin you wrote *to* in your response to the question on Fred d'Aguiar's "Letter to England" (p. 64). Write a letter back *from* that cousin to his cousin—you—in the Caribbean!

COUNTRY DAYS
Willi Chen (p. 92)

Line 3: "bovine"—of oxen, used to imply slowness or stubborn stupidity.

Line 8: "circumventing"—evasive, disguising its real purpose.

Line 11: "the Grassy's gleeful song"—'Grassy' is a country name for any ground bird, one that nests or feeds in the grass.

Line 13: "replete"—full of.

Line 14: "soughing"—a moaning, whistling sound.

Line 21: "verdigris"—literally a green cystalline substance that forms on the surface of copper after the action of acetic acid, but used in the poem to describe the colour and the growth of the moss.

Line 34: "frescoes"—pictures painted on a wall.

Line 35: "murals"—another kind of wall painting.

Line 42 & 47: "ochre"—a yellowish brown painter's colour—its precise tone depends on what its mixed with, so "dun-ochre" or "rust-ochre".

Line 46: "sienna"—an earth brown colour, important to artists painting landscapes.

Line 50: "incandescent"—glowing, shining brightly.

Line 63: "etched"—an artists' print-making technique in which a drawing is cut into a plate by the action of acid, but in the poem the children's toes cut a pattern into the sand.

Line 71: "russet"—a reddish-brown colour, the term applied usually to cloth or a particular type of apple. But the word also has associations of the rural and rustic generally.

Line 76: "scabrous"—in this context having a rough, broken kind of surface, but also with overtones of menace.

Line 78/9: "mahoe", "saman", "sandbox"—species of trees.

QUESTIONS

1 Willi Chen is an internationally renown painter and sculptor. Readers of his poetry have commented that he writes "with a painter's eye". What do you think that means? Find places in the poem where you are particularly aware of that "painter's eye".

2 Look at the following images in the context of the poem, what do you understand by them? How do they contribute to the overall atmosphere of the poem?
(a) "furrows of shivering cane"
(b) "ink-stained pitchpine desk tops/
Riddled, niched by scribing nibs"
(c) ". . . The sun's smothering lantern/
Lowered its wick . . ."

3 This poem is a kind of day-dream or a memory embroidered by the passing of time. Is there a time or a place that you use as a kind of "idylic" escape—it might even be a fantasy of the future? Write about it.

7: *Old Folks, Death and Grief*

INDIGONE
Edward Kamau Brathwaite (p. 96)

Title: "Indigone"
This poem is part of a sequence which links the colours of the rainbow with phases of life. So indigo, almost the last colour of the rainbow, becomes indigone, a poem about the end of life.

Line 1: "hoom"
In his notes to the poem Edward Kamau Brathwaite defines this as "an empty home" in the sense that "grandfather" is no longer there: it is a "memory of home".

Line 9: "cofflewalks"
A coffle is a line of animals or slaves fastened together.

Line 11: "joe louee with his powderpuff"
Joe Louis was a black American heavyweight boxing champion of the world in the 1930s and 1940s. His "powderpuff" is an ironic comment on his "soft dynamite boxing gloves" which decorated the face of his opponents. A powderpuff is a part of a woman's make-up kit, with which she applies powder to her face—it is the kind of thing you might buy in a general goods store—where this part of the poem is set.

Line 12/13: "the dionnese quin/ triplicates"
This refers to a Canadian family of children, all born on the same day, whose faces were used in advertisements for soap etc in the 1940s.

Line 15: "a rosicrucian EYE"
The Rosicrucians are a religious group, who believe in the existence of a "natural magic" and the power of symbols to focus believers' minds in order to draw on that power. The eye is one of their symbols. Traditionally it symbolizes the absolute power of God.

Line 19/20: "spinning dog"
The trademark of the *His Master's Voice* record company was the picture of a dog listening to an old-fashioned gramophone. This was printed on the centre label of all the records produced by that company (and at that time it was a leading label), so that as the record played the dog spun around.

Line 21–4: *"red sails in the sun/set/ when the roll and i'll be dead when you glad you rascal you"*
These are all lines from songs that were popular as 78s (the old style records) in the time that is being recalled. The last line should be "I'll be glad when you're dead, you rascal you", but the person remembering it has garbled the order of the words.

Line 23: "hoof"—hole.

Line 23–25: "okeh . . . victor . . . vox . . . bluebird . . . his master's vice (voice)"
These are all names of record companies of the period. The play on words with "vox trot" is intended to remind us of the foxtrot, a dance popular at that time.

Line 27: "ogun carved and cared for"
See the poem *Ogun* (page 14) for an account of the poet's carpenter/ sculptor uncle.

Line 28/9: "selassie's war"
Haile Selassie was Emperor of Ethiopia when Italy attempted to annex it in 1936.

Line 38: "betujels"
This is a phonetic version of Betelgeuse, a star in the constellation of Orion.

Line 41: "like quixote with his lance"
Don Quixote was the hero of a famous novel by the Spanish writer Cervantes in the seventeenth century. Don Quixote was an unworldly, rather foolish knight dedicated to defending honour—with his lance— wherever honour seemed threatened.

Line 68: "as i his sun"
The poet is interchanging "sun", the life sustaining force of existence, and "son", one means by which men (and women) defy mortality. Also the son/ sun is looking down at the corpse's upturned face.

Line 69: "i"
The i is not capitalized in this section of the poem because the lower case letter visually suggests the body of a man—the dot is his head, etc.

Line 73: "that ole rugged cross"
This refers to a hymn often sung at funerals.

Line 79: "articule"
This suggests "articles of faith".

Line 82: "megalleons"
Mega means super powerful; galleons are sailing ships; here space/time ships. Because of the words "storing up", the word also suggests gallons (of petrol).

Line 103: "crabs cassiopeas andromedas"
These are all the names of star systems, constellations and galaxies.

Line 104: "black lidded electronical caves"

This is a reference to the "black holes" of astronomy, mysterious pockets of outer space where normal laws of science do not seem to apply. Some people think the universe was created through the activity of these black holes. The image also calls to mind the black hole into which a coffin is lowered, and the "dark" eye of the skeleton.

QUESTIONS

1 The English poet Wordsworth once wrote that "The child is father of the man". Does this poem make any sense of that apparently paradoxical statement? If so, how?

2 Why, do you think, does the poet make so much use of a "cosmic" mythology in this poem?

3 This poem grows from a child's memory of his grandfather's funeral. Have you ever attended a funeral? Write about it, in whatever form seems most suitable—you might write a "report" as if for a newspaper, or you might use the funeral as the basis for a story, or you may want to write a poem about a funeral that was a particularly significant occasion for you.

CUT-WAY FEELINS
James Berry (p. 99)

QUESTIONS

1 Could this poem have been written as successfully, as poignantly, in Standard English? If not, why not?

2 What do you make of the use of the proverb that is the final line of the poem?

3 Using your answer to question 2, use that proverb as the title for a piece of writing of your own.

ALBERT
A L Hendriks (p. 99)

QUESTIONS

1 What is the speaker's attitude to Albert in the poem?

2 Identify and explain the examples of irony in this poem.

3 Write an account of the funeral and—briefly—the life that preceded it, as if you were Miss Vi. Use the information provided by the poem, but remember that the narrator may not be an objective reporter and that Miss Vi may see things very differently.

EARTH IS BROWN
Shana Yardan (p. 100)

Line 4: "dhoti"
This is a loin cloth worn by Hindus.

Line 37: "Hanuman"
He is the monkey god in Hindu mythology, who is the son of the wind and able to fly. He is a much respected and honoured deity.

Line 39: "logie"—a hut.

Line 41: "tabla"
This is an Indian musical form, a tune.

Line 51: "sitar"
It is an Indian musical instrument. Its strings are plucked rather than bowed.

QUESTIONS

1 It would seem that the dead man's grandchild, the speaker in this poem, is more understanding of the old man's ways than were his own sons. Do you agree? What evidence does the poem provide?

2 Do you think the grandfather in this poem has died, or is he still alive? What evidence do you have to support your view?

3 Issues around the "generation gap" are considered in this poem. Are you aware of differences in attitude to important things between your parents and your grandparents generation? I'm sure you will be aware of a gap between your view of things and your parents. Write about "The Generation Gap"; it would work well as a subject for a dialogue, but you may want to approach it another way, perhaps using "Earth is Brown" as a kind of model.

ON AN EVENING TURNED TO RAIN
Ian McDonald (p. 101)

Line 32: "old counterfeit Pharoah"
The Pharoahs were the rulers of ancient Egypt. When they died they were buried with all sorts of objects that might be useful on their journey to the afterlife, and with the symbols of their power so that they would be recognized and treated with appropriate respect. So the old sailor in his coffin with a lead name tag round his neck is a counterfeit—or false—Pharoah.

Line 68: "an echo of the saint's calm prayer"
The saint referred to whose prayer this is was Saint Augustine.

Line 76: "Gandhi in his hungering quest"
Mahatma Gandhi was the leader of the Indian struggle for independence in the 1920s, '30s and '40s. He believed in non-violent protest. He sometimes exerted moral pressure by going on hunger strike.

QUESTIONS

1 Why has the poet drawn our attention to the weather and the time of day in the title of this poem?

2 What do *you* think the old man meant by his last words?

3 Read this moving, disturbing poem again, at least twice. The living invest great significance in the last words of the dying, we say people don't tell lies on their

death-beds, confessions made "at death's door" as it were are invariably believed, but, as this poem demonstrates, last words are often ambiguous, their meaning open to great speculation and debate. Write a poem or story of your own titled "Last Words".

TERMINAL
Mervyn Morris (p. 103)

QUESTIONS

1 Why is the poem called *Terminal*?

2 Identify and explain the pun in line 14.

3 Why do some words in the poem begin with a capital letter?

4 Why have full stops/commas/semi-colons been omitted?

5 Examine the stanza breaks. If the poem were printed without stanza breaks, where, and in what ways, would its meaning be altered?

6 This poem says a great amount in less than 40 words. Allow yourself 40 words to write a poem about . . . you choose.

THEOPHILUS JONES WALKS NAKED DOWN KING STREET
Heather Royes (p. 103)

Title: "King Street"
This is the name of a busy street in downtown Kingston, Jamaica.

Line 12: "At Tower and King"
This refers to the Tower Street and King Street crossroads.

Line 26: "the green-rimmed palisades"
The airport in Kingston is on a long spit of land stretching out to sea. This stretch of land is known as palisadoes.

QUESTIONS

1 Why did the carwash boys call Theophilus Jones "'Madman'" (line 13)? Is he mad? Justify your answer by reference to the poem.

2 In what sense is Theophilus Jones's final walk down King Street "his triumphant march" (line 7)?

3 In what sense is Theophilus Jones "letting himself go" (line 27)?

4 "There is a certain dignity in the death of Theophilus Jones." Discuss.

5 By using the date of the event as the opening line the poet is both locating the events that follow in time and suggesting that this was just another day, nothing particularly notable about it to provoke Theophilus Jones action. The events of any given day can be dramatic and memorable, but the "ordinariness" of any day can be material for poetry too. Take yesterday's date and day of the week as the first line of a poem of your own. If nothing startling or out of the ordinary happened write about five routine events of the day as vividly as you can.

simple tings
Jean Binta Breeze (p. 104)

QUESTIONS

1 What do you understand by the following phrases in the context of the poem?
   (a) "miles of travel in her store"
   (b) "read the rain signs
       in the sky
       evening's ashes
       in a fireside"
   (c) "de simple tings of life"

2 How does the language used to narrate the poem contribute to its success?

3 Write a poem of your own titled "The Simple Things of Life" (or "de simple tings of life" or any other formulation of the same words in a creole appropriate to your self or your subject).

THE SADDHU OF COUVA
Derek Walcott (p. 105)

Title: "saddhu"
This is a religious title meaning Holy Man.

Title: "Couva"
This is the name of a village in Trinidad.

Line 16: "mantras"
A mantra is a kind of prayer, a chant or a song that aids meditation.

Line 17: "Anopheles"
This is the scientific name for one kind of mosquito.

Line 17: "sitar"
See note on line 51 of *Earth is Brown* (page 100).

Line 18: "Divali"
This is the Hindu Festival of Lights, which is held at the end of the Hindu year in honour of Lahshami, the goddess of prosperity.

Line 21: "Ramayama"
This is the name of a holy book of the Hindu faith. It takes the form of a poem some 24,000 verses long telling the story of Rama—a reincarnation of the god Vishnu—and his wife Sita.

Line 24: "Bengal"
This is a region of north-east India, part of which is in what is now Bangladesh.

Line 25: "Uttar Pradesh"
This is a state in northern India through which the River Ganges—sacred to Hindus—flows.

Line 51: "the snake-armed God"
This probably refers to Naga-Sanniya, who is a Hindu deity with power over nightmares. However, many of the Hindu gods are traditionally depicted with "snaking" arms.

Line 52: "Hanuman"
See note on line 37 of *Earth is Brown* (page 100).

QUESTIONS

1 How would you describe the tone of this poem?

2 Explain what is implied in: "There are no more elders./Is only old people" (lines 43–4).

3 How could "all the gods" be "killed by electric light" (line 54)?

4 What would the Saddhu of Couva have in common with the grandfather mourned in *Earth is Brown* (page 100).

5 The poem begins and ends with images of the sunset; look at them again. Think of other images for the sunset. A spectacular sunset can be an inspiring event, but it is also—as the moment between light and dark—an important "marker" in the passage of the day for people who wouldn't think of sitting on a beach and watching it sink into the sea. Write a story or a poem "about" the/a sunset or in which a sunset plays an important part in the unfolding of the plot.

MAMMIE
E A Markham (p. 107)

QUESTIONS

1 Where is Mammie living now, do you think?

2 What does the poet mean when he speaks of Mammie's "—now unnecessary—age" (lines 6–7)?

3 Why is she "pleased/he was not the father of her sons" (lines 21–2)?

4 The old woman in this poem has a story to tell about her past. All old people have stories they could tell, many have lived through experiences and changing times that you would find it hard to imagine. If they are around, ask your grandparents to tell you a story from their past. Otherwise try and get another elderly person from your district to speak to you. Write the story as they tell it, or use it as the basis for a story of your own.

HOT SUMMER SUNDAY
A L Hendriks (p. 107)

QUESTIONS

1 What is the main way that Grandpa in the second stanza differs from Grandpa in the first stanza?

2 Why does it say in the poem: "it seemed he might stir" (line 19)?

3 Identify and explain the pun and the paradox in "straightly lying" (line 14).

4 "The phrase 'straightly lying" (line 14) is crucial to the meaning of the poem." Discuss.

5 What images comes into your mind when you think of a hot summer Sunday? Write about them.

THE ORDERING OF ROOMS
Dennis Scott (p. 108)

QUESTIONS

1 What are the rituals or activities that particularly remind the narrator of the poem of his mother? Why are they so poignant for him?

2 What do you understand by the last two lines of the poem?

3 Think of the "small" things your mother—or grandmother/aunt/ whoever looks after you at home—does for you all the time, that you perhaps take for granted. Make a list of them. See if you can use that list as the basis of a poem of your own.

8: *Gods, Ghosts and Spirits*

OL' HIGUE
Wordsworth McAndrew (p. 110)

Title: "Ol' Higue"
This is a creature of Guyanese folklore, an old woman who removes her skin at night and flies out of her house disguised as a ball of fire. She hovers near the home of her intended victim, usually a baby or small child, and when the child is asleep, flies in and sucks its blood—often until it dies. Tradition has it that Ol' Higue must return from her evil forays before day break. It is also believed that chalk marks and blue garments will protect babies against her, and that a bowl of rice will distract her attention as she will be compelled to count the grains.

Line 5: "swizzly"—wrinkled.

Line 18: "goobi"
This a mortar (as in mortar and pestle) where Ol' Higue traditionally hides her skin while she is out on her evil rounds.

Line 19: "semidodge"—swerve.

Line 21: "dutty-powder"—stained.

Line 28: "jalousie"—shuttered window.

Line 34: "tikkay"—beware.

Line 43: "asafoetida"
This is a strongly scented plant often used in herbal medicine.

Line 57: "Whaxen! Plai!"
These are words mimicking the sounds of sticks and kicks beating flesh.

Line 62: "mancicole"—baton.

QUESTIONS

1 In your own words, explain in detail how the Ol' Higue got caught.

2 Who speaks in lines 63–4?

3 What is onomatopoeia? Identify two examples of it in this poem.

4 What is the narrator's attitude to Ol' Higue? Is the narrator mainly sympathetic to her, or hostile, or neutral? How do you know?

5 "The Ol' Higue gets what she deserves." Discuss.

6 Ol' Higue is a particularly Guyanese figure, but most countries have their equivalent witch-vampire figures. What figure from your island's folklore most closely approximates to the Ol' Higue? See if you can write a poem about "her", taking the shape as well as the spirit of Wordsworth McAndrew's wonderful poem as a model.

SHABINE ENCOUNTERS THE MIDDLE PASSAGE
Derek Walcott (p. 112)

Title: "Shabine Encounters the Middle Passage"
This is a section of a much longer poem, *The Schooner Flight*. The speaker, Shabine, is a sailor on an inter-island schooner, *Flight*. On a foggy morning he encounters this vision.

Line 14: "barkentines"
A barkentine is a kind of sailing ship with three masts.

Line 18: "Shabines"
In this context it means sailors, like the speaker, whose nickname is Shabine.

QUESTIONS

1 Line 7 reads "it was horrors, but it was beautiful". How can that be?

2 In what ways can you relate the last stanza of this poem to a poem by Walcott which appears earlier in this anthology?

3 This poem wonderfully evokes and embroiders on that experience of seeing shapes or figures in the mist that may or may not be there which most of us have experienced on misty mornings. The idea of shadowy figures, half seen and half imagined is a haunting one . . . use it to set the scene for a ghost story of your own.

LEGEND
Faustin Charles (p. 113)

QUESTIONS

1 What do you understand by the following lines or images from the poem
(a) "After an exorcism by the priest"
(b) "Old ebby initiated and entered a crab's skull"
(c) "Like father, like son
Melting in the crab-nerve,
Fused into one."

2 . . . One night when the moon was full . . . the *obeah-man* who lives on the hill. . . . Write a story beginning from here.

COUVADE
Victor D Questel (p. 114)

Title: "Couvade"
This is an Amerindian custom, shared with several other peoples across the world, according to which the *father* of a new born child is put to bed—perhaps for two weeks—and treated as if he were physically affected by the birth process. The word is derived from the French "couver", meaning to hatch or incubate.

QUESTIONS

1 How would you describe the "atmosphere" of this poem?

2 What did you make of this poem the first time you read it, before you had seen the note above?

3 What, in a paragraph, would you say the poem is "about"?

4 What traditions surround the birth of a child in your community? Some birth rituals are formal and traditional, reflecting social attitudes towards either parent or the child, others have become customary and are more informal . . . how did your father celebrate your birth? Was your mother treated in a special way in the period following the birth? Write about it, either as if writing a feature for a magazine or use any ideas/images that emerge from your discussion and research to write a poem or story.

ROLLIN'-CALF
Louise Bennett (p. 115)

Title: "Rollin-Calf"
This is a demonic creature of Jamaican folklore and superstition. The *Dictionary of Jamaican English* defines it as a "monster taking the form of a calf with fiery eyes, and haunting the road and countryside at night. People who lead dishonest or wicked lives are said to turn 'rollin' calf' when they die."

Line 1: "Meh deh pon hase, me cyaan tap now"
I'm in a hurry, I can't stop now.

Line 7: "You mussa hear seh Tahta laas'—You must have heard that Tahta lost.

Lines 19/20: "me/Tan a yard an hear de lick"—I stood in my own yard and could hear the sound of him beating the cow.

Line 23: "Him see de sinting two yeye-dem" He saw the something's two eyes.

Line 33: "Bra Caleb"—Brother Caleb.

Line 36: "Him dissa twis an foam."—His mouth is all twisted and foams.

Line 39: "yeye"—eye.

Line 40: "ketch"—catch one, come back with one.

QUESTIONS

1 Do you believe in ghosts and ghouls?

2 What does the form of the poem—the regular rhythm pattern, the rhymes, the end stopped lines and verses—

contribute to the overall manner of the poem? Written another way this could be a really sinister and terrifying story, why isn't it so here.

3 Try and write a poem in ballad style similar to this one relating any experiences you have had, or stories you have heard on such subjects.

KORABRA
Edward Kamau Brathwaite (p. 116)

Title: "Korabra"
The Korabra is a funeral drum of the Ashanti people in what is now Ghana. The word means, literally, "go and come back".

Line 14: "kra"—soul.

Line 23: "Elmina"
This is the name of a notorious fort on Ghana's Cape Coast which was a centre for the despatch of slaves on their journey to the Caribbean.

Line 41: "kenkey"
This is a kind of food made with cornmeal wrapped in leaves.

Line 44: "Asofaskye"
This is the name of the warriors of the tribe.

Line 62: "Akuapim"
This is a region of Ghana, homeland of the speaker.

Line 64/5: "Nyame's tree"
This was one of the names of the great Creator God of Ashanti belief, who was said to have made the three realms of the universe: the sky, the earth and the underworld. His symbol

is a three-forked "tree" which holds a gourd containing thunderstones.

Line 67: "Nazarene's Cross"—the cross of Jesus. The "symbol" of the Christian god.

Line 69: "the gong gong"
This is the name of the metal chime or ball which proceeds the drum through which the gods speak.

Line 82: "Koforidua"
This is the name of a holy tree, symbol or residence of an angry god.

QUESTIONS

1 What do we know about the person who speaks in this poem?

2 Where is he speaking from?

3 What sort of journey is he undertaking?

4 Identify and explain any four of the puns signalled by dividing a single word into two.

5 This is a poem about a journey of the spirit after death. Many peoples—of many faiths and none—believe in an afterlife of some kind, of a spirit world, of this kind of journey of the spirit . . . What do you believe about these things? How do you feel about the journey the poem takes us on? Can you discover what other people in your own community or country believe about the afterlife? Write about it, either as if writing a feature for a magazine or use any ideas/ images that emerge from your discussion and research to write a poem or story.

UNCLE TIME
Dennis Scott (p. 117)

QUESTIONS

1 Identify six comparisons made in this poem, and assess the appropriateness of each.

2 What is a metaphor? What is a simile? Identify in this poem one example of each.

3 Thinking about time and the inevitability of death, make up metaphors and similes appropriate to your particular surroundings to express those ideas. They are traditionally represented in such figurative language, i.e. Old Father Time, the Grim Reaper etc. See if you can expand or extend those images to make a poem.

HELLO UNGOD
Anthony McNeill (p. 118)

QUESTIONS

1 Would you call this poem a kind of prayer?

2 What "picture" of Ungod do you get from phrases such as "testing 123" and "disconnecting"?

3 What do you think lines 3–4 mean (a) literally, (b) metaphorically?

4 What do you think line 11 means (a) literally, (b) metaphorically?

5 Why is there a stanza break after line 19?

6 This poem has a feeling of the Apocalypse—the end of the world—about it. In its short, stark, frantic statements and questions it suggests an imminent calamity . . . How, why, when might "the end of the world" come about? Some religious faiths anticipate that ending in various ways . . . can you discover what they are? But the fear of the man-made destruction of the planet is one that crosses all barriers of faith and circumstance, ranging from ecological abuse of the planet's resources to terrible visions of nuclear or chemical warfare. Many writers have been inspired to write about "The End of the World" . . . add your story to theirs.

FRACTURED CIRCLES
James Berry (p. 118)

QUESTIONS

1 What aspects of this poem suggest to you that it might be read as a kind of spell?

2 Examine the structure of the first nine stanzas (down to line 27). In what ways are these stanzas alike?

3 In what ways does the final stanza (lines 28–30) differ in structure from the previous nine?

4 What do you think is being suggested by "a green man/ wandered from white sheets" (lines 26–7)? What positive associations does the word

"green" have in this context? What negative associations do the words "white sheets" have in this context?

5 Why is the poem called *Fractured Circles*?

6 What riddles or recipes or "spells" do you know? Write them down. Can you make up any others? Can you shape them and arrange them so that they become more like poetry? Try.

PARISH REGISTERS
John Gilmore (p. 119)

Line 4: "Morocco"—a kind of fine, flexible leather.

QUESTIONS

1 This is a poem about history. What does the poet mean when he says "No other monument have these/whose labour built our land"?

2 Consider the use of the following images
(a) "gleam like wedding rings in duppy dust"
(b) "heaps of paper, blotched and mottled/as the freckled features of an overseer"
(c) "the door is shut upon their muted voices"

3 Think about the image of the "muted voices" of the people listed in the registers. Try and "free" one of those voices—tell a story in the voice of one of those characters—Susan or John or Martha or Peter.

MOONGAZA
Rooplal Monar (p. 120)

Title: "Moongaza"—is another awesome figure from Guyanese folklore

Line 5: "loco-line"—train line.

QUESTIONS

1 Tell the story of "Moongaza" in your own words.

2 How does the way the poet tells the story contribute to its effectiveness? Think about the kind of language he uses, the kinds of incidents he uses to tell us about "Moongaza" and the use of questions, repetitions and exclamation marks.

3 "The Night I Saw Moongaza" . . .

SUN POEM XV
Wilson Harris (p. 121)

QUESTIONS

1 What does "visionary" (line 8) mean? Would you call this a visionary poem?

2 What is implied by the word "now" in line 11?

3 Would you say this is a poem about death, or creative vision, or both?

4 "Although the poem positively acknowledges the dark underground life of growing trees, most of its images point towards creative space and light." Discuss.

5 Write a "Sun Poem" of your own.

9: *Her Story*

SAD MOTHER BALLAD
Jane King (p. 124)

QUESTIONS

1 Find out what a ballad is. What kinds of subjects are traditionally dealt with in ballad form? Why do you think the poet chose that form for this poem?

2 In the context of the poem as a whole, what do you understand by the following images,
(a) "but I want to give them stone"
(b) "my thoughts are like sea serpent"
(c) "mermaid songs it once had uttered"

3 Try out the ballad form for yourself—the subject can relate to this poem or be of your choosing. Read the poem aloud a couple of times to establish a sense of the rhythm and the way the rhymes work.

CROWN POINT
Velma Pollard (p. 124)

Line 10: "penny-royal"'—a scented species of mint, used in herbal medicine.

Line 13: "Khus Khus"—a sweet scented grass used for perfumes, fans etc.

QUESTIONS

1 The title and first stanza of the poem seems to suggest a place to locate the inspiration for the poem. How do you read that first stanza? What do you make of the word "hupentery".

2 Why does the narrator feel that her grandmother's spirit is not usually able to make such certain contact with her? What are "my tomorrows' spaces".

3 Is there a special place you go to try and sort out your thoughts, to "open" yourself in the way the narrator does in the poem? Write about it.

OF COURSE WHEN THEY ASK FOR POEMS ABOUT THE "REALITIES" OF BLACK WOMEN
Grace Nichols (p. 126)

Line 64: Self-negating—to deny one's own existence.

QUESTIONS

1 The poet suggests two contrasting images of black women's experience, the "abused stereotype" and the "perfect song"—what do you understand by the two images?

2 Is the poem saying, finally, that there is essentially no difference between the experience of black women and women of other colours/histories? Do the last two stanzas apply equally to white woman or green women?

3 What is a stereotype? Are stereotypes always harmful? Try and imagine—or recall—a situation in which a stereotype is used to judge someone. Write a story about it.

OARS
Mahadai Das (p. 127)

QUESTIONS

1 The poem makes comparison between words and oars. How does the poet extend and develop the metaphor? How effective a comparison does it seem to you?

2 What do you notice about the structure of the poem? Each unit is a closed, complete unit—piled one upon another. What effect does that structure have in terms of the way the poem "moves"?

3 What metaphor would you choose or develop for your feeling about words? For some people they are real "enemies"—treacherous, slippery, cold. For others they are precious tools of self-expression. Try and white a short poem about "words" employing that kind of metaphor.

I AM BECOMING MY MOTHER
Lorna Goodison (p. 127)

QUESTIONS

1 Part of what makes this poem work is the way the poet combines or contrasts mundane images against more "fantastic" images. Do you agree? Identify the images and discuss your responses to them.

2 What do you understand by the lines:
"and stored lace and damask tablecloths
to pull shame out of here eye."?

3 What can the narrator of the poem—or the poet—mean by "I Am Becoming My Mother"? Write a poem of your own that deals with the relationship between yourself and your mother or father.

THE LESSON
Merle Collins (p. 128)

(The following notes were provided by the poet to the published version of this poem)

Line 49: "Carib"—The Callinagos, the indigenous peoples virtually exterminated by the Europeans when they took the Caribbean countries. Carib, first used as a derogatory term for the Callinagos, is the name by which the indigenous people are now generally known.

Line 53: "Toussaint"—Toussaint L'Ouverture, black Hatian revolutionary leader, of the late 18th century.

Line 159: "Fedon"—Julien Fedon, leader of the 1795 Granada uprising against the British.

Line 161: "Theophilus Albert Marryshow", Grenadian journalist, trade unionist and politician, known as the "father" of the idea of Caribbean Federation.

Line 162/3: "Tubal Uriah Buzz Butler"—Grenadian who was at the forefront of the political, social and economic struggles in the Trinidad oilfields in the 1930s.

Line 171: "Fidel"—Cuban president Fidel Castro.

Line 174: "PRG"—People's Revolutionary Government of Grenadian, 1979–83.

Line 205/6: "Kay sala se sa'w"—Grenadian Patwa, translated in the final two lines. Patwa is a language spoken by some of the older people in Grenada and more widely spoken in St. Lucia, Dominica, Martinique and Guadeloupe. It is a result of African rhythms and speech structures combined with the French colonial experience.

QUESTIONS

1 Why, do you think, is the poem laid out the way it is? What is the effect of the short lines?

2 Comment on the passage from line 107—"Den/Me blood/run cole . . ."—to Line 134—"A little too fast". Notice the wit with which the poet uses the images of cold. What do you understand by the final six lines of that section of the poem?

3 Write a ten line poem of your own entitled "History". (Or if you'd rather, "Herstory".) Think about the story the poem tells— how notions of what history *is* have changed.

WITHOUT APOLOGY TO PROUST
Christine Craig (p. 130)

Title: "Proust"—Marcel Proust, nineteenth century French novelist best known for *Remembrances of Things Past*, which is, perhaps, what is being referred to here.

Line 6: "Nanny"—(poet's note) Nanny was a Maroon leader, the only woman to be named among Jamaica's national heroes.

Line 6: "Sheba"—The Queen of Sheba, a biblical character, (See I Kings 11) a woman of great power and splendour,—supposed to be the ancestral mother of the kings of Ethiopia.

Line 8: "Erzulie"—African/New World goddess of love and fertility, from the pantheon of the Fon people of what is now Benin.

Line 8: "Diana"—Roman mother-goddess and goddess of the hunt.

QUESTIONS

1 In what sense can "Sheba and Nanny, (be) riding/laughing through her cells"? Are they related?

2 What do you make of the image spread over lines 12–17, from "A sleeping girl. . . ." to "for her quiet ear". What is the effect of the line break between "grains of/ possible . . ."?

3 Observe, or conjure up in your mind's eye, the picture of a child sleeping. What associations are brought to your mind? Try and write a poem around them?

STILL MY TEACHER
Rajandaye Ramkissoon-Chen (p. 131)

QUESTIONS

1 Read in one way the older woman's gift to her former pupil isn't much to get excited about— a battered old book of poems, not even a new one. Why is the narrator of the poem so moved and inspired by the book?

2 What do you understand by the image in the final three lines of the poem?

3 Has there been a particular teacher who has inspired you to try and make the most of your talents? Write a pen portrait of him or her.

soun de abeng fi nanny
Jean Binta Breeze (p. 132)

Title: "Abeng"—see note to line 144 of "The Land of Look Behind", (p. **155**).

Line 1: "Nanny"—see note to line 6 of "Without Apologies to Proust".

Line 23: "cockpit"—The "cockpit country" is the name given to the land the Maroons claimed and held against the British in the heart of Jamaica. See note to "The Land of Look Behind", (p. **155**).

Line 32: "dutty tuff"—the ground is hard.

Line 52: "de wattle an de daub"—mud walled houses.

QUESTIONS

1 Notice the use of rhyme in this poem and the repetition of the lines "dutty tuff/but is enuff/fi a bite/fi we fight. How do those two devices—rhyme and repetition—contribute to the overall effect of the poem?

2 What do you feel about the way the language is shaped—and even the way it is spelled—to suggest a particular voice? What does it suggest to you about the "performance" of the poem—would it be more effective read aloud than silently off the page?

3 This is a kind of praise poem—a poem honouring a distinguished figure in the community. It is a "public" rather than a private or personal poem. Try and write a praise poem to honour a public figure from your country's past, or present if you prefer. Try and avoid the stock empty phrases of political rhetoric and public speaking.

WHEN HE WENT AWAY
Peggy Carr (p. 134)

QUESTIONS

1 Consider the images in the third stanza of the poem. Identify them, and write about the ways they reinforce each other.

2 This is a poem about love and exile but seen from the point of view of someone left behind. How does the final stanza bring the issues together and comment on the whole "story"?

3 Write a poem or story of your own called "When He (or She) Went Away"—it can refer to anyone, friend, parent, brother/sister or public figure.

THE LOADED DICE
Amryl Johnson (p. 135)

Title: "Loaded Dice"—the term has various associations but two seem particularly relevant to the poem; dice are said to be "loaded" if they are unfairly weighted in such a way as to make it more likely that particular faces will come up when the dice is rolled. In another sense events are said to be loaded when a great deal depends on their outcome—so, much may hinge on the way these particular dice fall.

Line 4: "When dey divided Africa . . ." At the end of the nineteenth century, and again after the first World War, the European colonial powers divided Africa up between them. So the British, for example, took control of West African countries now called Nigeria, Ghana, Sierra Leone and The Gambia. The boundaries between the countries drawn on the map of the continent were arbitrary but the consequences of that division have been long lasting and often unforeseen.

QUESTIONS

1 What do you think actually "happens" in this poem? Who says the final line? Is there more than one "speaker" in the poem?

2 What is the effect of the repetition of the first line of the poem so many times?

3 Think about the notion of "loaded dice". Write a story in which significant events turn on the roll of a set of dice or similar chance events.

TO MY ARAWAK GRANDMOTHER
Olive Senior (p. 136)

Line 6: "Yokahuna"—an Amerindian goddess.

Line 7: "Coyaba"—the Arawak word for heaven.

QUESTIONS

1 The first line of the poem is a startling image. What can the poet mean by it? How do the lines that follow help to "explain" it?

2 What do you understand by the final three lines of the third stanza? Is it telling the reader something about the occasion of the poem's inspiration?

3 Ideas of ancestry are important in many places but perhaps especially in the Caribbean where slavery, indenture and migration has been such a feature of the region's history and broken so many family connections. See if you can find a copy of Vera Bell's wonderful poem of the 1950s— "Ancestor on the Auction Block"—and look at several of the poems in the "Roots" section of this anthology. Think about your own family history—what you know for certain or can find out from elder relatives. Then think about what you don't know. Write a poem or story about your own ancestors, real or imagined.

10: *Exile and Homecoming*

NIGGER SWEAT
Edward Baugh (p. 138)

QUESTIONS

1 Who is the poem addressed to? Is it a story that is actually "told" or does it takes place in the mind of the narrator? What is your evidence for this? How does the last line turn much of the rest of the poem on its head?

2 Considering the language of the poem and the things the narrator "says", what sort of person might s/he be?

3 I think this poem is a kind of "secret narrative", something the person says under his breath "against" authority. Everyone makes up these kinds of "counter" stories when facing a teacher or parent or policemen etc. Using your own experience as a starting point, set the scene and write a story where such a "secret narrative" plays a part.

THERE RUNS A DREAM
A J Seymour (p. 139)

Line 2: "Guiana"—before Independence the country now called Guyana was known as British Guiana.

Line 5: "Stellings"—landing stages.

QUESTIONS

1 Who were the "strong and quiet men" who "drove back a jungle, gave Guiana root"? Why is this a "dream"?

2 What do you understand by the phrase "History moved down river?"

3 The image of the forest creeping back "foot by quiet foot" is very powerful, the forest reclaiming its lost territory. In one sense that's obviously a literally "true" image, but it is also a metaphor for the process of reclamation in other dimensions of experience.
Explore that metaphor in a piece of writing of your own.

MIDSUMMER, VII
Derek Walcott (p. 140)

Line 9: "palanquins"—a kind of covered bed or chair, carried—like a stretcher—by men at each corner.

Line 21: "Thomas Venclova"—the dissident Czech writer

Line 22: "Heberto"—perhaps Heberto Padilla the dissenting Cuban poet?

QUESTIONS

1 What impression of the place he describes does the poet create in lines 1–14?

2 After line 14 the tone of the poem changes. What issues does the poem raise in that final section? What do you understand by the lines
(a) "One step over the low wall, if you should care to, recaptures a childhood whose vines fasten your foot".
(b) "exiles must make their own maps".
(c) ". . . when this ashphalt takes you far from the action, past hedges of unaligned flowers?

3 The idea of nostalgia for a place once known is central to the sequence of poems this piece is taken from. If you have ever moved from a place, or stopped going to a place you often visited as a child—to visit relations perhaps—try and write a description of it and include some sense of how you felt about the place.

THE SEA
E A Markham (p. 141)

QUESTIONS

1 Why is this poem called "The Sea"? What does the sea "stand for" in the narrator's life? How do you understand the final line of the poem?

2 Poems, like people, employ different tones of voice. We all know how a word spoken in one tone of voice can mean something very different. Take the word "really", for example. How does the tone of voice in which the word is used change its meaning? How would you describe the tone of this poem? How does it contribute to the "meaning" of the poem?

3 Invent a character of your own who uses a similar tone of voice. Write him/her a passage of dialogue.

AEROGRAMME
Phillip Nanton (p. 141)

Line 13: "autopsy"—an operation performed after death to determine the cause of death. Sometimes lines are drawn on the body to guide the surgeon making the incisions.

QUESTIONS

1 Several words in the poem ascribe "human" features and feelings to the aerogramme. What are they? What is the effect of that process of anthropomorphising?

2 Find the image of the stamp on the envelope. How has the poet made that familiar, insignificant object seem "strange" and so, interesting?

3 The "literal" way of looking, of describing, that you note in your answer to question 2, can be applied to all sorts of objects to make them interesting to a reader. Take any object out of your pocket. Look at it hard for a while. Describe it as if you had never seen anything like it before, as if you didn't know what it was for or where it came from.

COOLIE ODYSSEY
David Dabydeen (p. 142)

Title: "Coolie"—a slang term for a person of Indian descent.

"Odyssey"—originally the title of an epic poem by Homer describing the journey and adventures of Odysseus—now the word is used to mean a quest or any long journey. So the title refers to the journey from India to Guyana and from Guyana to Britain that members of the family in the poem have made.

Line 24: "old Dutch plot"—the rest of the poem is set in Guyana, which was once a Dutch colony and still retains some Dutch influence in its language and architecture etc.

Line 27: "Ramadhin"—Sonny Ramadhin was a great West Indian spin bowler in the 1950s.

Line 31: Balham—a district in London.

Line 44: Albion was an ancient name for Britain—there quite probably is an Albion village in Guyana, but the poet is playing on the irony of the name in relation to the narrator's journey's to and from "Albion".

Line 53: "Lord Krishna"—one of the great deities of Hinduism.

Line 78: "catechist"—a preacher, not formally qualified as a priest but competent in the oral promulgation of church teaching.

Line 92: "King George's Town"— now Georgetown, the capital of Guyana.

Line 93: "El Dorado"—see note to Mark McWatt's poem "Porknocker", p. **000**.

QUESTIONS

1 In the overall context of the poem what do you understand by the lines

"Folk that know bone
Fatten themselves on dreams
For the survival of days"?

2 There are several locations in this poem. Identify them. The poem shifts back and forth between these locations and in time. How do those shifts work in terms of telling the story?

3 Consider the idea of an odyssey or quest in terms of your own family history—just about everyone in the Caribbean got here as a consequence of some ancestor's journey, and many people have relatives who have travelled on to other parts of the world. Write a story or a poem that begins from that idea of an Odyssey. You don't *have* to attempt to write an epic poem, but on the other hand even Homer had to start somewhere!

GROUND
John Robert Lee (p. 146)

QUESTIONS

1 Look up and read Psalm 127 in the Bible; how does it affect your understanding of the poem?

2 Note how the formality of the poem's language changes towards the end. What does that change suggest to you? How do you feel about words like "trodding"? What exactly does it mean, do you think? What would be the effect of substituting that translation for the word in the poem?

3 Take a story from the bible—or another holy text—and remembering the way John Robert Lee responds and adapts his source material in "ground"— use it as the basis for a piece of writing of your own.

STEREOTYPE
John Agard (p. 147)

Line 59: "Anthropology"—the study of human behaviour.

QUESTIONS

1 What are stereotypes? How many does John Agard identify in the poem? Who would hold such stereotypical images? Is it such a person that the narrator is speaking to?

2 This poem uses wit and humour to make a very serious point, but there aren't any "jokes" as such, are there? How does the humour come across then? What is the point being made in the final stanza?

3 We all use stereotypes to some degree. Discuss in groups your images of other "categories" of people—for example, tourists, Englishmen, Africans, other islanders, teachers, people who compile poetry anthologies . . . ! Stereotypes are only really dangerous and harmful if we "believe" them unquestioningly and apply the negative notions they often contain to individuals. Do you agree? Trying to use humour, write a poem that makes use of stereotyped attitudes.

RAMON REMEMBERS
Wayne Brown (p. 148)

Line 11: "expurgation"—to purify or make clean.

QUESTIONS

1 There is a Biblical echo to the story of this poem—do you think it refers to the journey of the Magi or not? What is your evidence for that judgement.

2 What sort of person is Ramon? How do you know? What do you understand by the final stanza?

3 This poem draws on a memory that has haunted the narrator for a long time—something he saw but didn't quite understand. Such flashes of memory are often very vivid, even if the circumstances around them are not. Write about a memory of your own that stays with you from childhood, even though you may not be quite sure of its context or "meaning".

RETURN
Dionne Brand (p. 149)

QUESTIONS

1 At first this seems like a purely descriptive poem, an intense scrutiny of a place once known, but it is also a very judgemental poem, the language is far from neutral. Would you agree?

2 What is the effect of using just that one word as the final line of the poem?

3 ". . . still the hard, distinct, brittle smell of slavery." Use that line as the opening line of a story.

WHEREVER I HANG
Grace Nichols (p. 150)

QUESTIONS

1 What impression of England do you get from the poem? What does the narrator mean when she says she has changed her "calypso ways"?

2 Much of the poem has a rather melancholy tone, a sadness, but this is undercut by the humour of the final line—do you agree?

3 If you could travel to a foreign country to live for a while—or even for good—where would you choose to go? Why? What do you think the place would be like? How do you know? Do you think you would be home sick? Write about it.

MAI VILLAGE
Edward Kamau Brathwaite (p. 151)

Title: "Mai"—My.

Line 2: "sauters"—Sauters is a village in Grenada where the Amerindian people leapt over the cliffs to their deaths rather than be captured and enslaved by the Europeans.

Line 2: "six mens bay"—Six Men's Bay is a fishing village in Barbados, site of an ancient Amerindian settlement.

Line 10: "marcus malcolm martin and mahatma"—references to black anti-colonial and civil rights leaders, Marcus Garvey, Malcolm X, Martin Luther King and Mahatma Ghandi.

Line 15: "kwashiorkor"—a tropical disease of children, caused by a lack of protein in the diet.

Line 17: "jean rhys . . . coulibri"—Jean Rhys was a famous West Indian writer, her best known novel *Wide Sargasso Sea* is set, in part, on a plantation called Coulibri.

QUESTIONS

1 "small, delightfully unspoiled the guide books say"
To some extent the poem is written "against" those lines—do you agree?

2 What do *you* feel about the way the poet avoids using capital letters, runs some words together, breaks others up and generates "new" expressions like "politricks" and 'boys will be boils" . . . What do you think the poet hopes to achieve by such devices?

3 Lots of poets have experimented with language in the kinds of ways Edward Kamau Brathwaite does in this poem—sometimes for sound effects, sometimes for political effect, sometimes for the sheer fun of playing with language. Try out your own experiments with making/breaking language from its traditional shapes, sounds and constructions.

INDEX OF POETS AND POEMS